AF411481

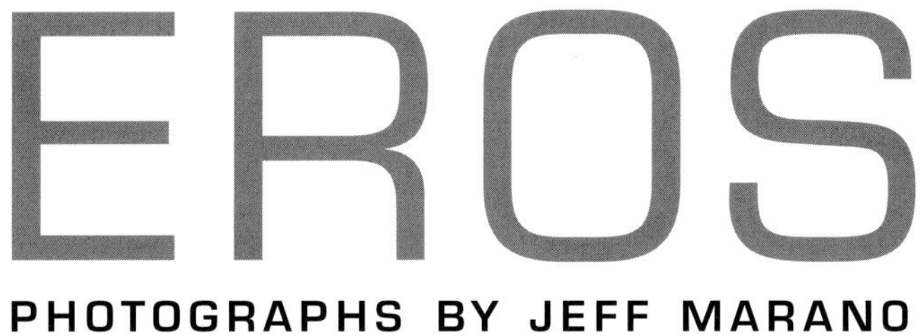

EROS

PHOTOGRAPHS BY JEFF MARANO

EROS

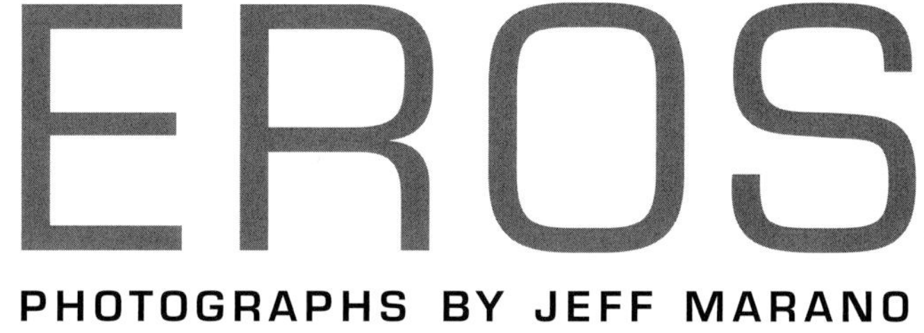

PHOTOGRAPHS BY JEFF MARANO

teNeues

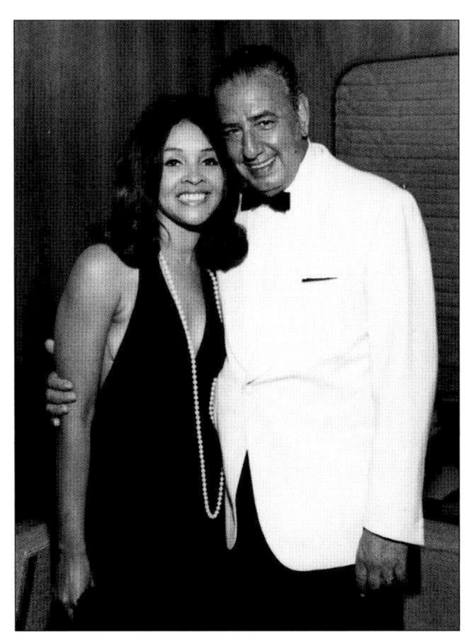

This book is dedicated to my mother SHIRLEY MARANO who was always there for me until the end. She always taught me "you are your own best friend" and if you don't believe in yourself no one else will. I will always be thankful for all of the love and powerful energy she embedded in me! I know she'd be proud!

I also dedicate this book to HERB RITTS for giving me my big model break back in June of 1983. For treating me like such a professional in a kind and unintimidating way. Herb was the expert on making you feel like a million! His inspiration was and still is insurmountable!!!

Jeff Marano, my friend... true entrepreneur of style, fashion photography and achievement! As noted author, A. Jackson King, once wrote, "The secret of every man who has ever been successful lies in the fact that he formed the bait of doing those things that failures don't like to do." Jeff is the eptimone of selecting goals that others can not achieve and does everything well!

Fashion and art have been the driving force for his confident direction. He started in the industry as a fashion model in New York then internationally, gracing the runways of such noted designers as Lanvin and Balmain to name a few. He was also photographed by famous photographers such as Herb Ritts and Matthew Rolston. Because of this experience and exposure with fashion, he decided to pick up a camera to capture the sensitivity of the soul, through the lens of his creative energy.

One of the remarkable things about the photos in this book is not just the power and beauty of work that was intended to be essentially erotic, but the fact that each model selected was allowed to have their own personality shine through. The assumption is that the reader would recognize the remitting devotion to the masculine form as art and not as an object.

STEVEN CUTTING
New York, fashion designer

Jeff Marano, mein Freund ... ein wahrer Unternehmer in Sachen Stil, Mode-
fotografie und Erfolg! Der berühmte Autor A. Jackson King schrieb einmal: „Das
Geheimnis jedes erfolgreichen Mannes liegt darin, dass genau die Dinge ihn rei-
zen, vor denen weniger erfolgreiche Menschen zurückschrecken." Jeff ist die
Verkörperung dieses Satzes: Er setzt sich Ziele, die für andere unerreichbar sind,
und reüssiert!

Mode und Kunst sind die Antriebskräfte, die ihn selbstsicher auf seiner Bahn
vorantreiben. Er begann seine Karriere als Model – zunächst in New York, später
auf internationalen Laufstegen. Dabei arbeitete er für so bekannte Designer
wie Lanvin und Balmain, um nur ein paar Beispiele zu nennen. Er arbeitete auch
für berühmte Fotografen wie Herb Ritts und Matthew Rolston als Model. Diese
Erfahrungen und Auseinandersetzungen mit der Modewelt veranlassten ihn
dazu, selbst die Kamera in die Hand zu nehmen und mit seiner kreativen Energie
die Verletzlichkeit der Seele einzufangen.

Die Fotos in diesem Buch zeichnen sich nicht nur durch ihre Aussagekraft und
Ästhetik aus, die im Wesentlichen erotischen Charakter hat, sondern auch da-
durch, dass jedes Model die Möglichkeit hat, die eigene Persönlichkeit mit einzu-
bringen. Die Folge davon ist, dass der Leser die männliche Gestalt hier als Kunst
wahrnimmt und nicht als Objekt.

STEVEN CUTTING
New York, Modedesigner

Jeff Marano, mon ami ... véritable entrepreneur dans les domaines du style, de la photographie de mode et de la création ! Un auteur de renom, A. Jackson King, a écrit que « le secret de la réussite réside dans le fait de trouver le moyen de faire ce que les perdants n'aiment pas faire ». Jeff a le don de choisir des buts que d'autres sont incapables d'atteindre et réussit tout ce qu'il entreprend !

La mode et l'art ont été le moteur d'une vocation toute tracée. Il fit ses débuts dans l'industrie en tant que mannequin à New York, puis, à l'échelon internatio-nal, en venant rehausser les défilés de maisons aussi célèbres que Lanvin et Balmain, pour ne nommer que quelques-unes. Il a été photographié par d'illus-tres photographes comme Herb Ritts et Matthew Rolston. Fort de ses expérien-ces dans la mode, il décida de prendre à son tour un appareil photo pour capter à travers son regard d'artiste la vulnérabilité de ceux qu'ils photographient.

Ce qui distingue notamment les photos de ce livre, ce n'est pas seulement la force et la beauté d'une œuvre essentiellement érotique, mais aussi la person-nalité de chacun des modèles qu'il laisse transparaître. Le but est que le lecteur comprenne sa vision de la forme masculine comme art et non comme objet.

STEVEN CUTTING
New York, styliste de mode

Jeff Marano, amigo mío... ¡un verdadero emprendedor en cuestión de estilo, fotografía de moda y éxito! El conocido autor A. Jackson King escribió una vez: "El secreto del hombre de éxito está en que le atraen justo las cosas que asustan a los hombres de menos éxito." Jeff es la encarnación de esta frase: Él se pone metas que para otros son inalcanzables ¡y triunfa!

La moda y el arte son las fuerzas impulsoras que lo hacen avanzar por su camino seguro de sí mismo. Comenzó su carrera como modelo, primero en New York, luego en las pasarelas internacionales. En esto trabajó para diseñadores tan importantes como Lanvin y Balmain, por sólo citar un par de ejemplos. También fue modelo para fotógrafos famosos como Herb Ritts y Matthew Rolston. Estas experiencias y la dedicación al mundo de la moda lo indujeron a tomar él mismo la cámara en la mano y atrapar con su energía creadora la vulnerabilidad del alma.

Las fotos de este libro se caracterizan no solamente por su fuerza expresiva y su estética, que esencialmente posee un carácter erótico, sino también por que todos los modelos tienen la posibilidad de aportar su propia personalidad. Se presupone que el lector reconoce que la forma masculina se percibe aquí como arte y no como objeto.

STEVEN CUTTING
New York, diseñador de moda

Jeff Marano, amico mio... un vero imprenditore per quanto riguarda lo stile, la fotografia di moda e il successo! A. Jackson King ha scritto: "Il segreto di ogni uomo di successo è che ha preso l'abitudine di fare proprio le cose che non piace fare ai falliti". Jeff è l'incarnazione di questa frase: si pone degli obiettivi che per altri sono irrealizzabili, e li raggiunge!

Sono state la moda e l'arte a spingerlo, sicuro di sé, sulla sua rotta. Ha iniziato la carriera come indossatore a New York, poi alle sfilate internazionali di noti stilisti come Lanvin e Balmain, per fare solo qualche nome, e posando anche per fotografi famosi, come Herb Ritts e Matthew Rolston. Queste esperienze e contatti con il mondo della moda l'hanno spinto a prendere in mano la macchina fotografica per catturare, attraverso la lente della sua energia creativa, la sensibilità dell'anima.

Una delle particolarità delle fotografie di questo libro è che non hanno soltanto la forza espressiva e la bellezza di un'opera essenzialmente erotica, ma anche il fatto che ognuno dei fotomodelli scelti ha avuto la possibilità di far trasparire la sua personalità. Si suppone che chi sfoglierà il libro riconosca che le forme maschili vengono celebrate come arte e non come oggetto.

STEVEN CUTTING
stilista, New York

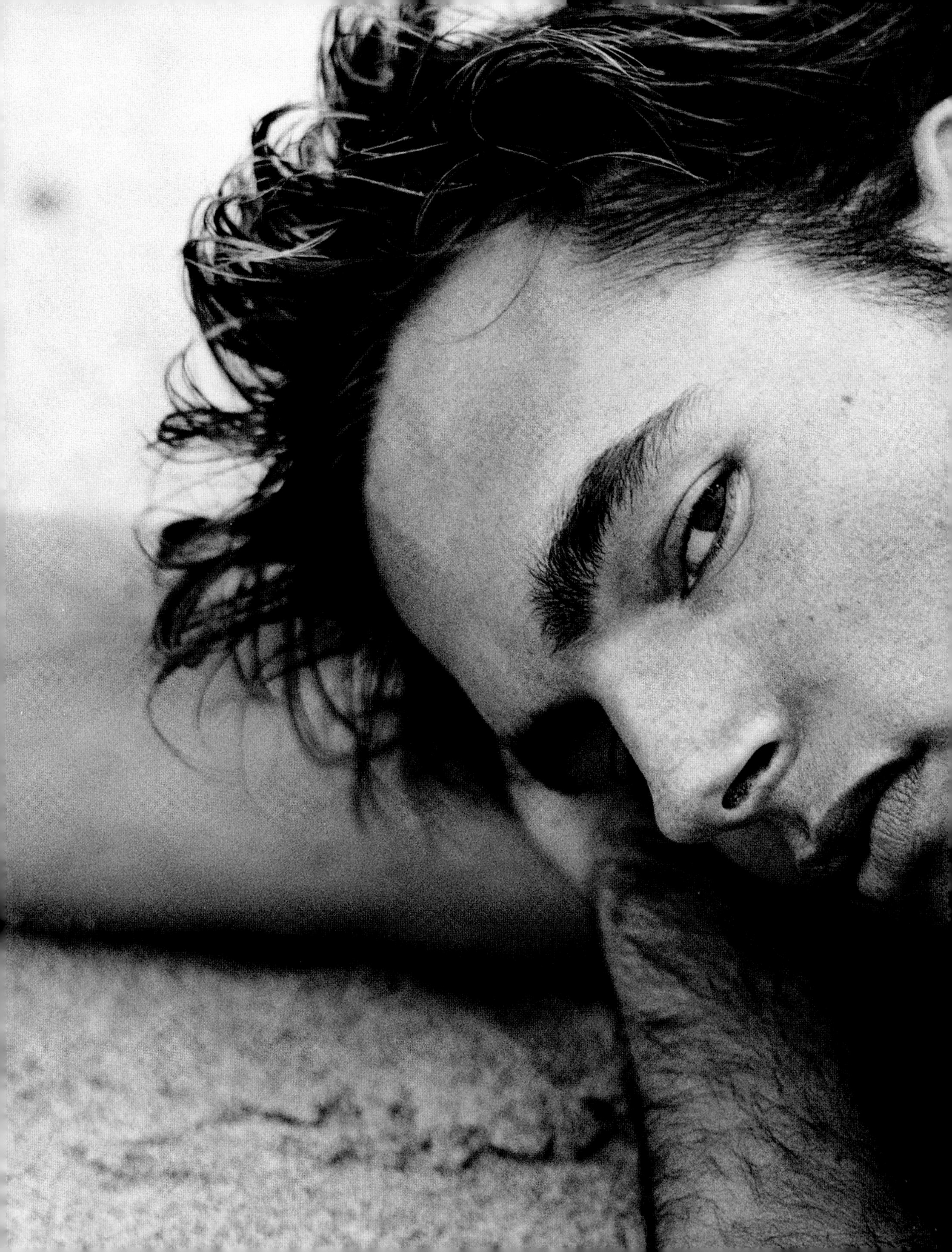

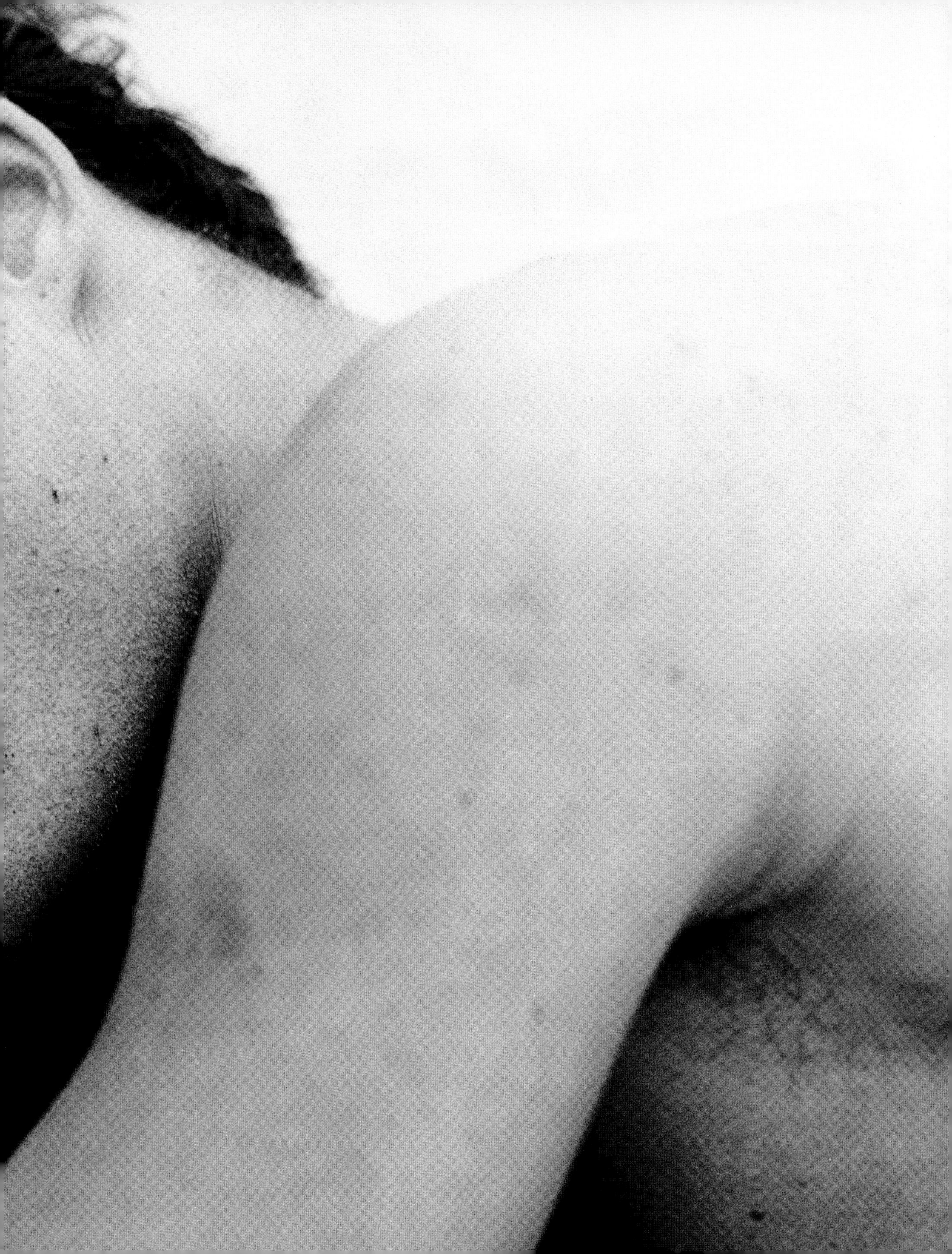

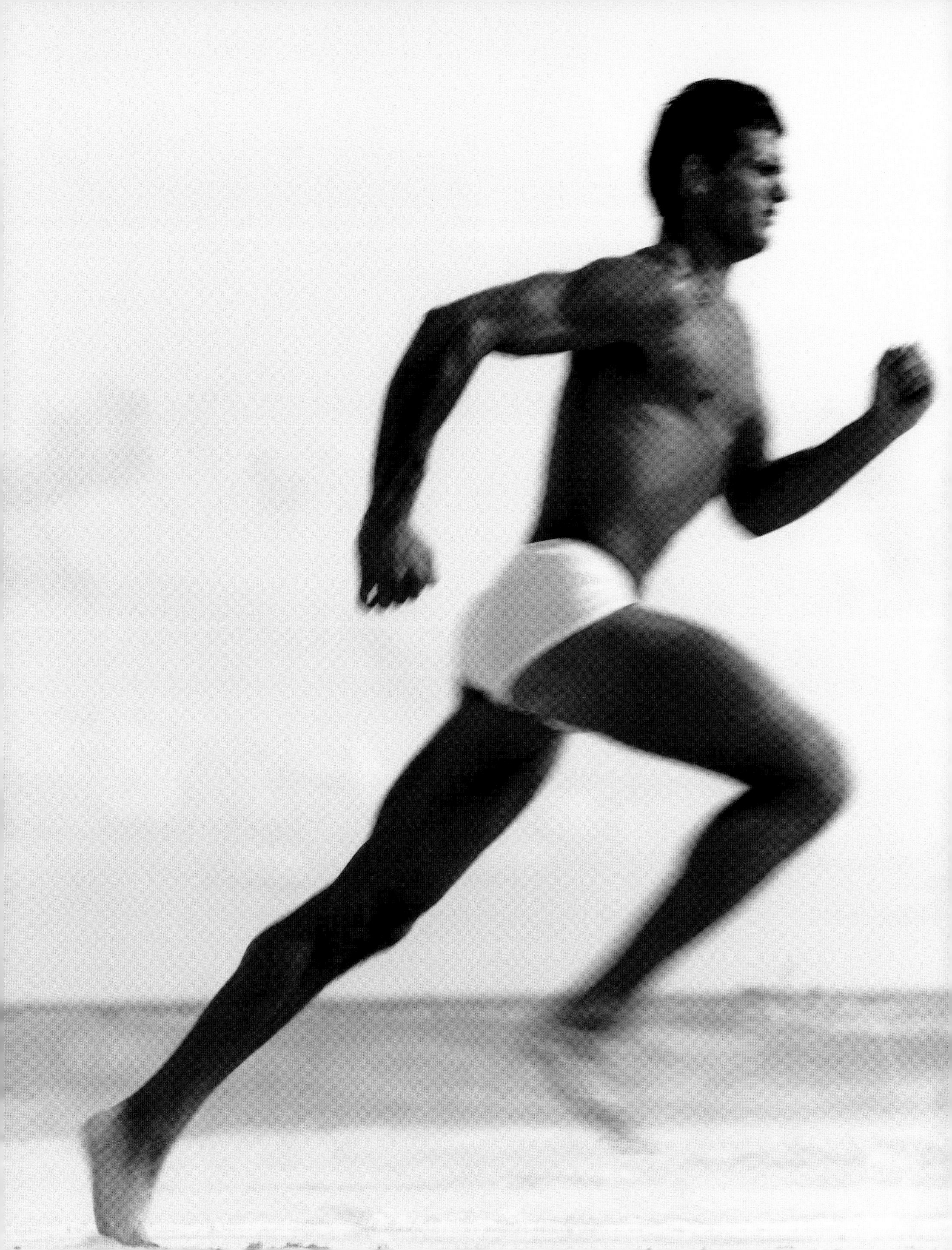

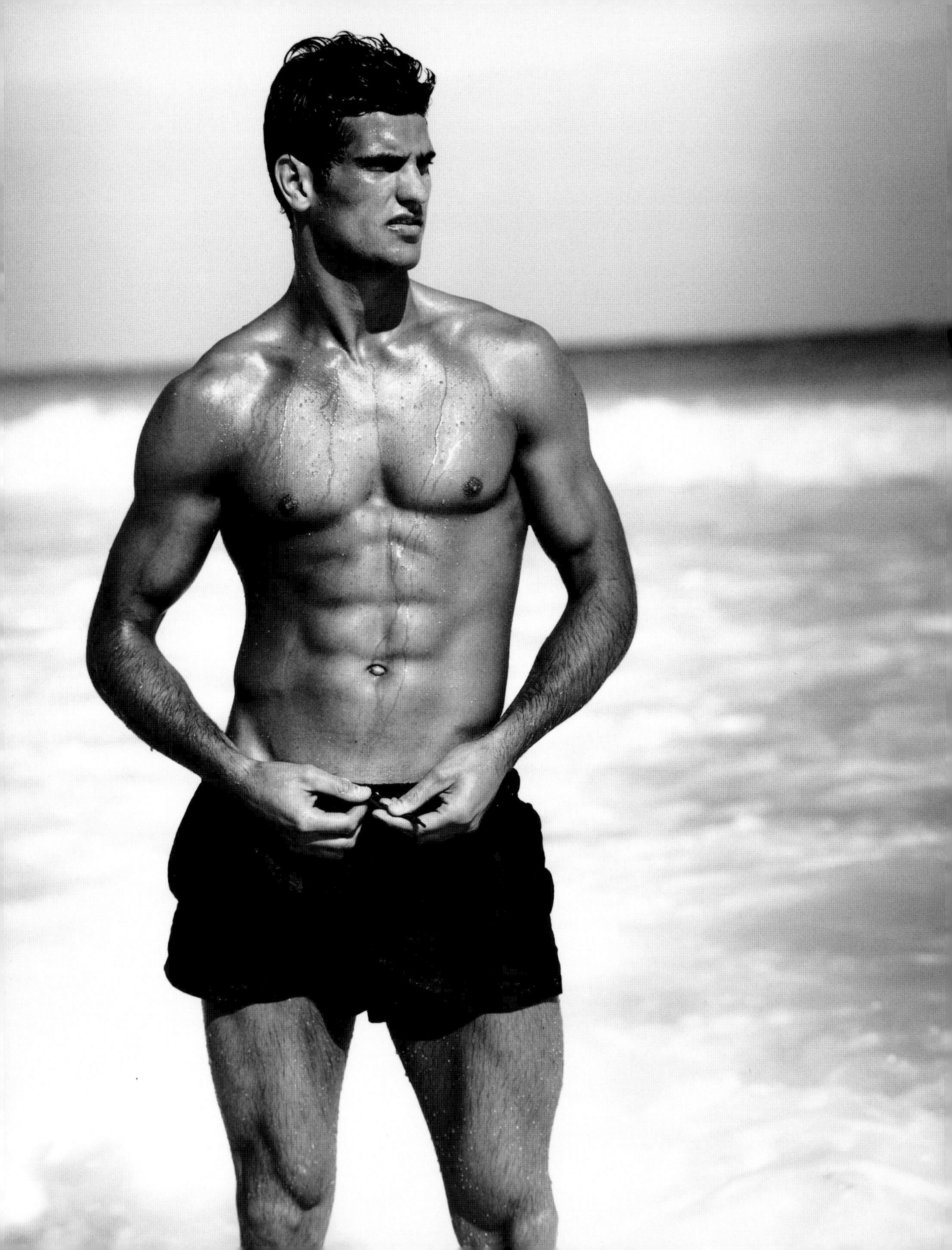

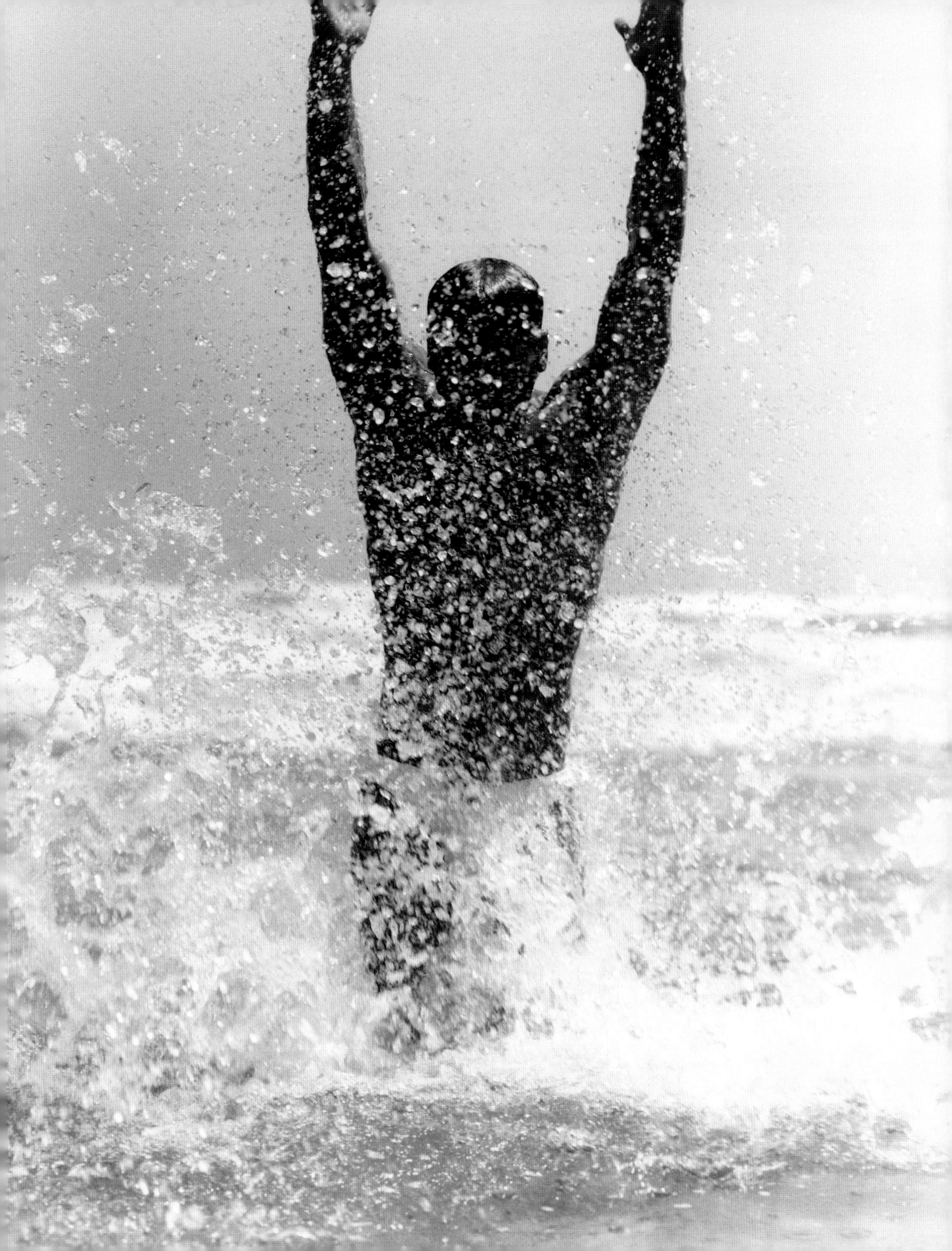

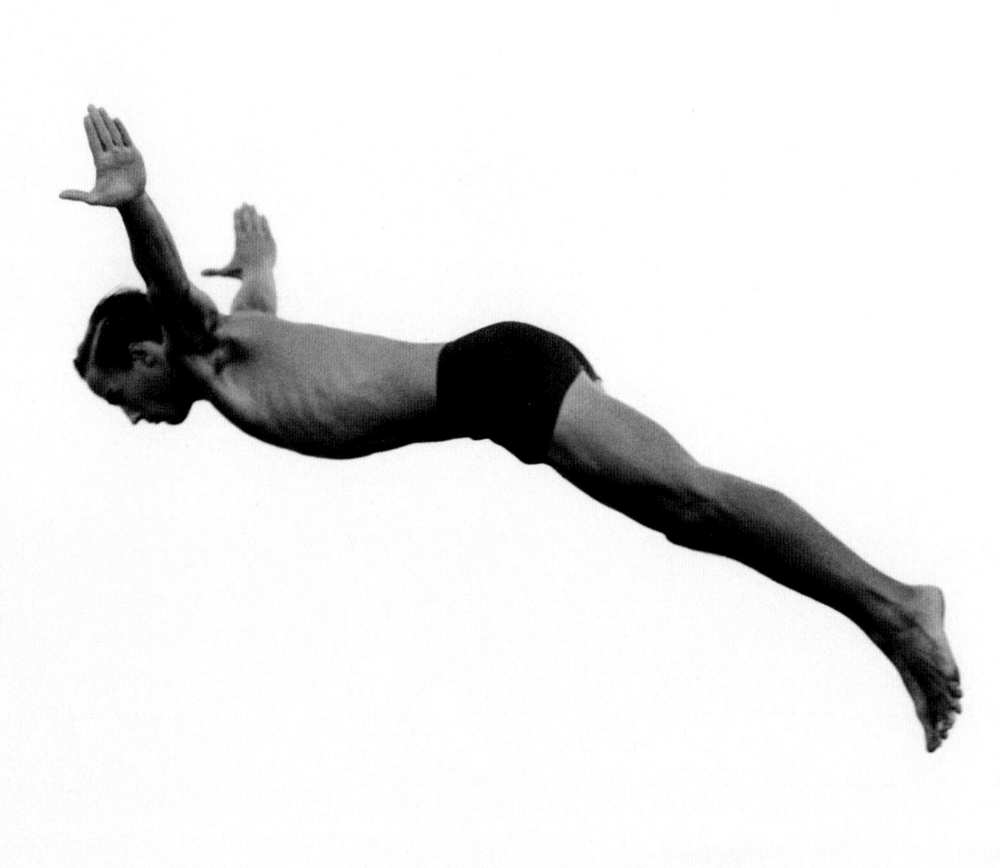

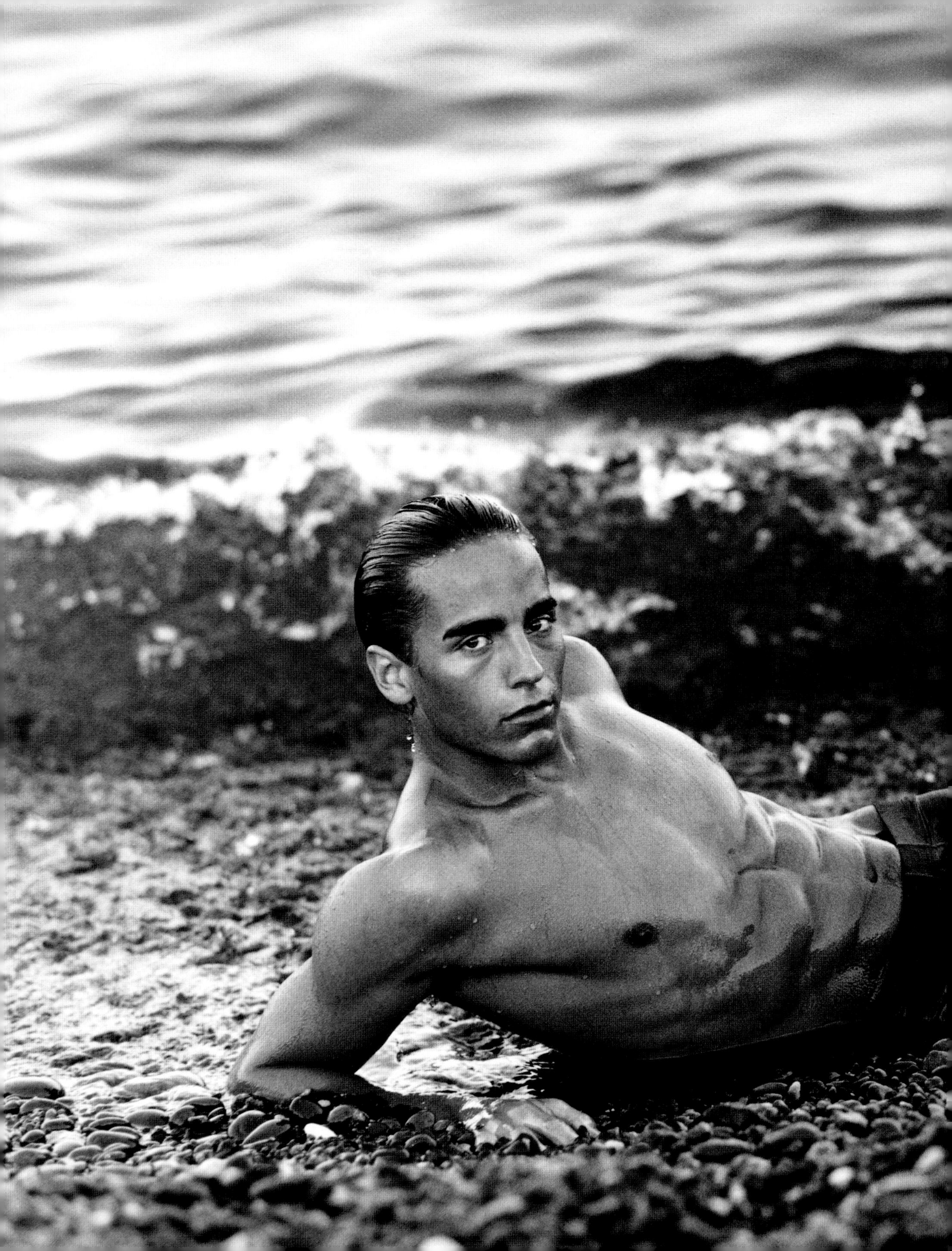

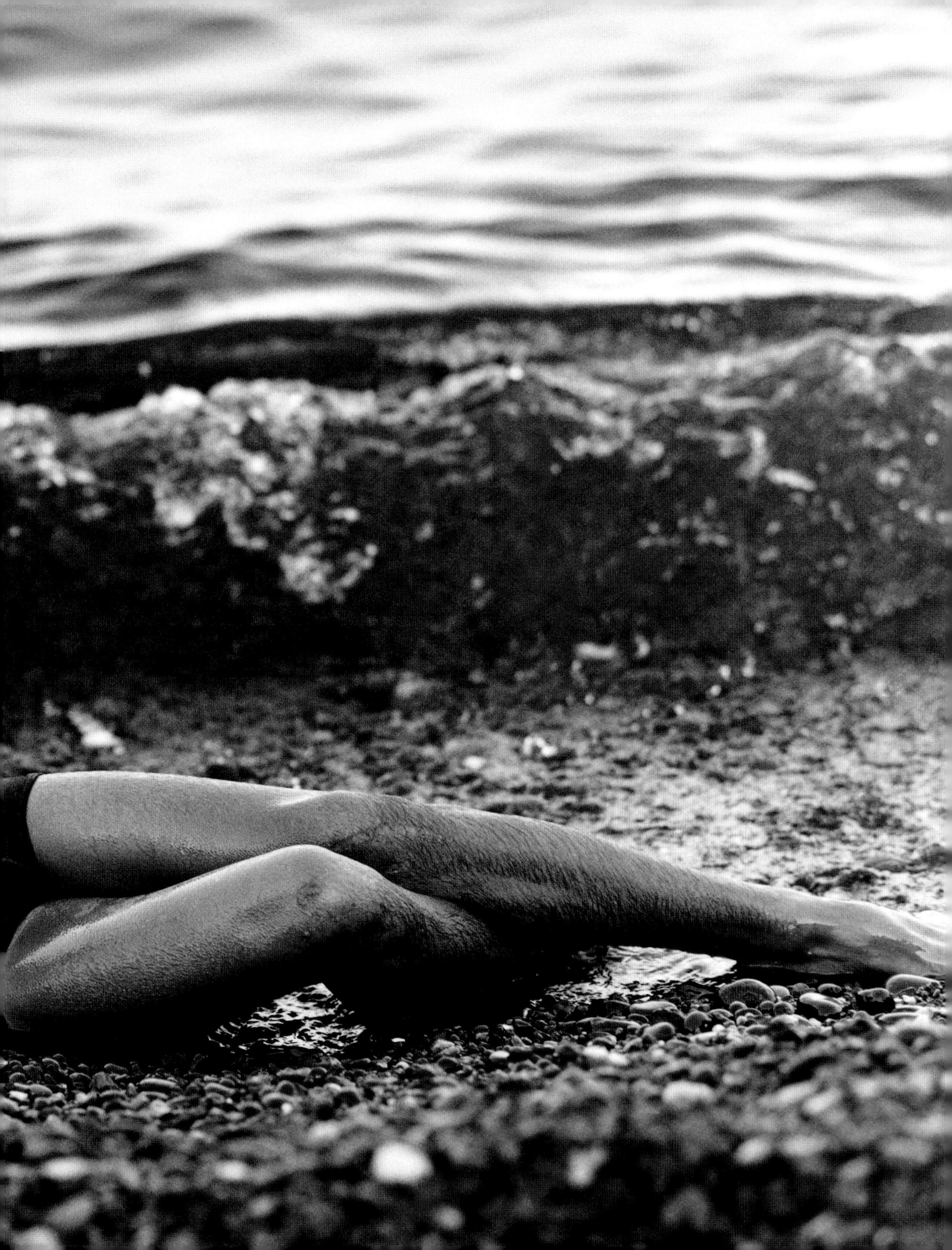

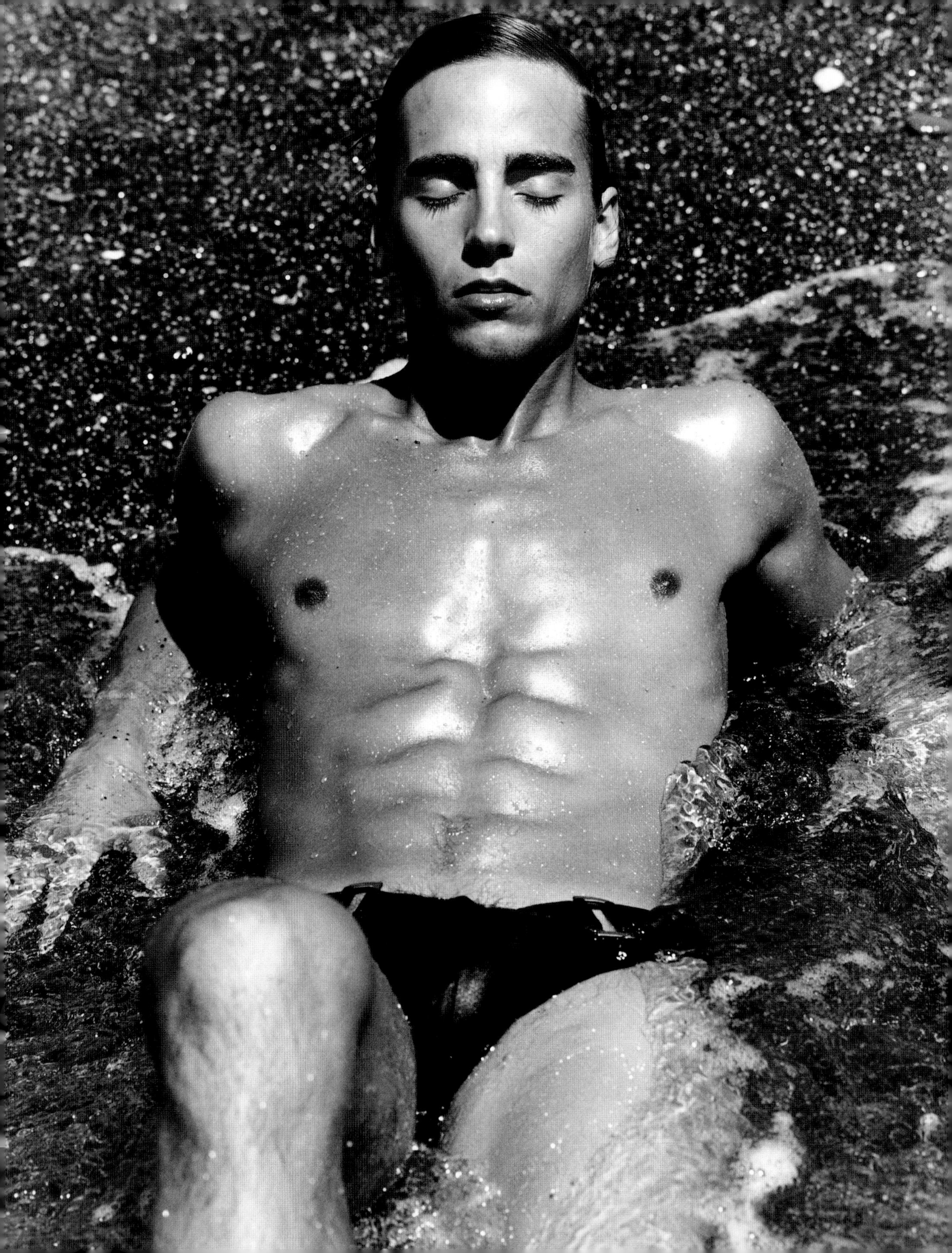

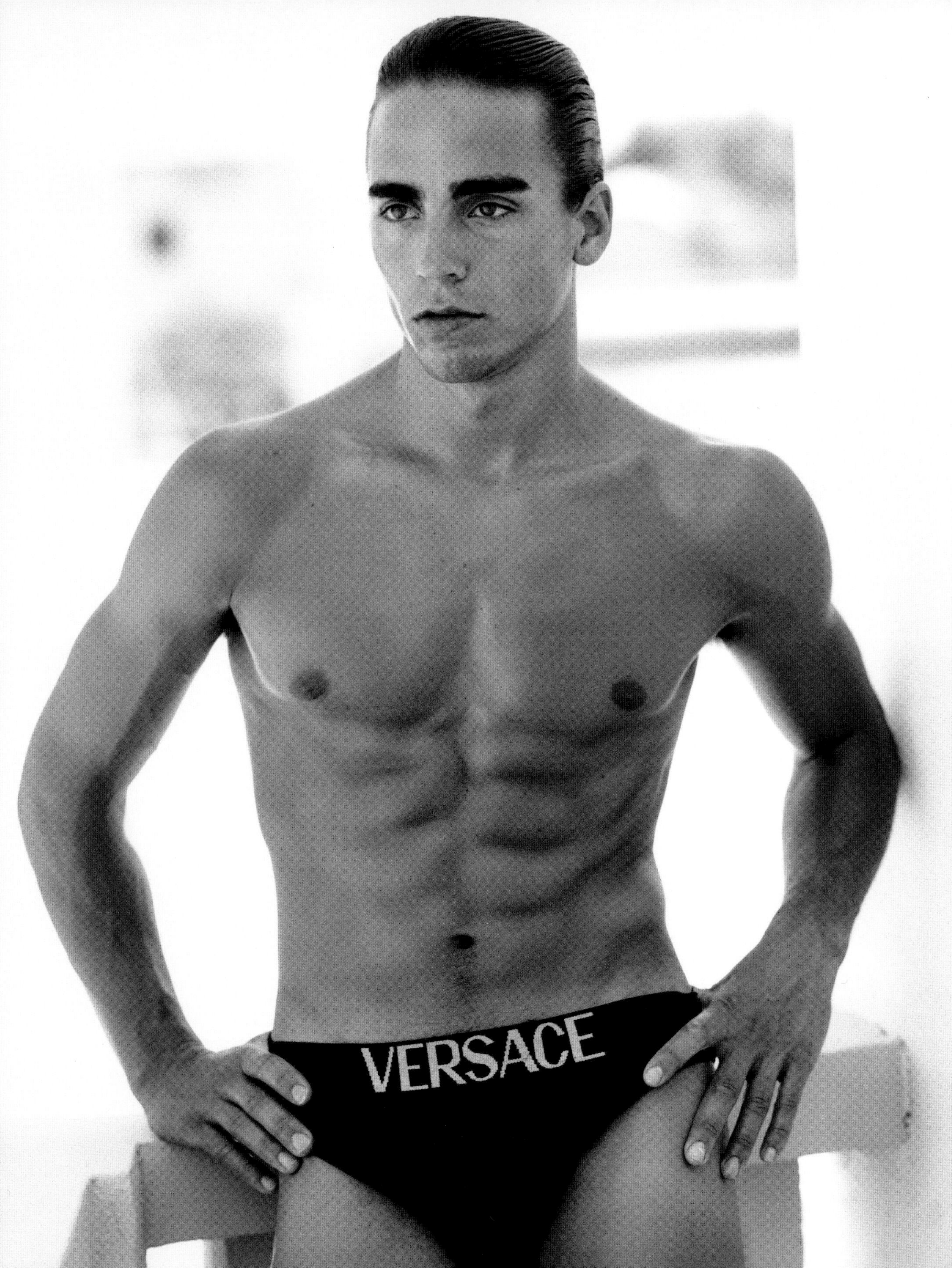

VERSACE

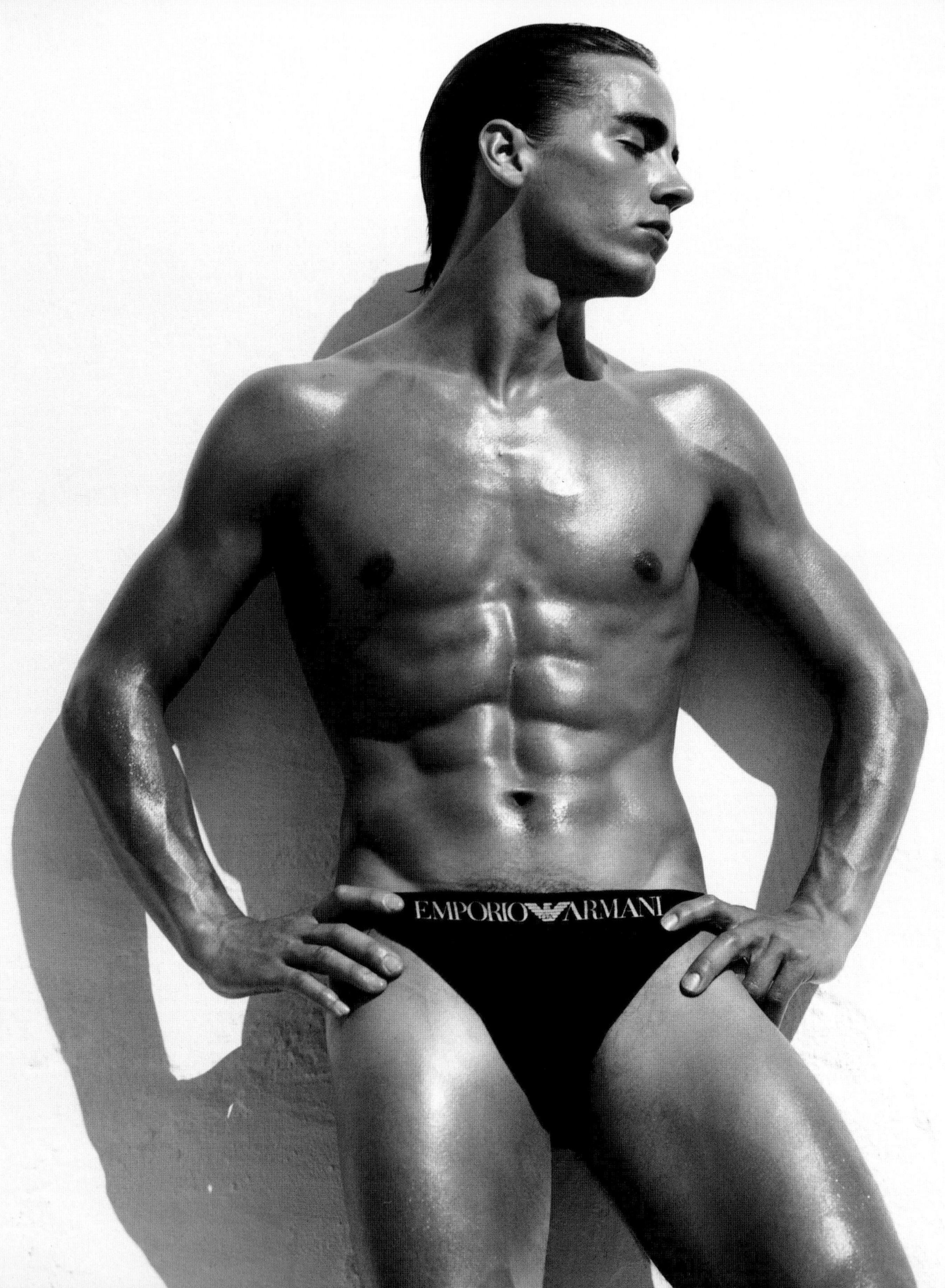

EMPORIO ARMANI

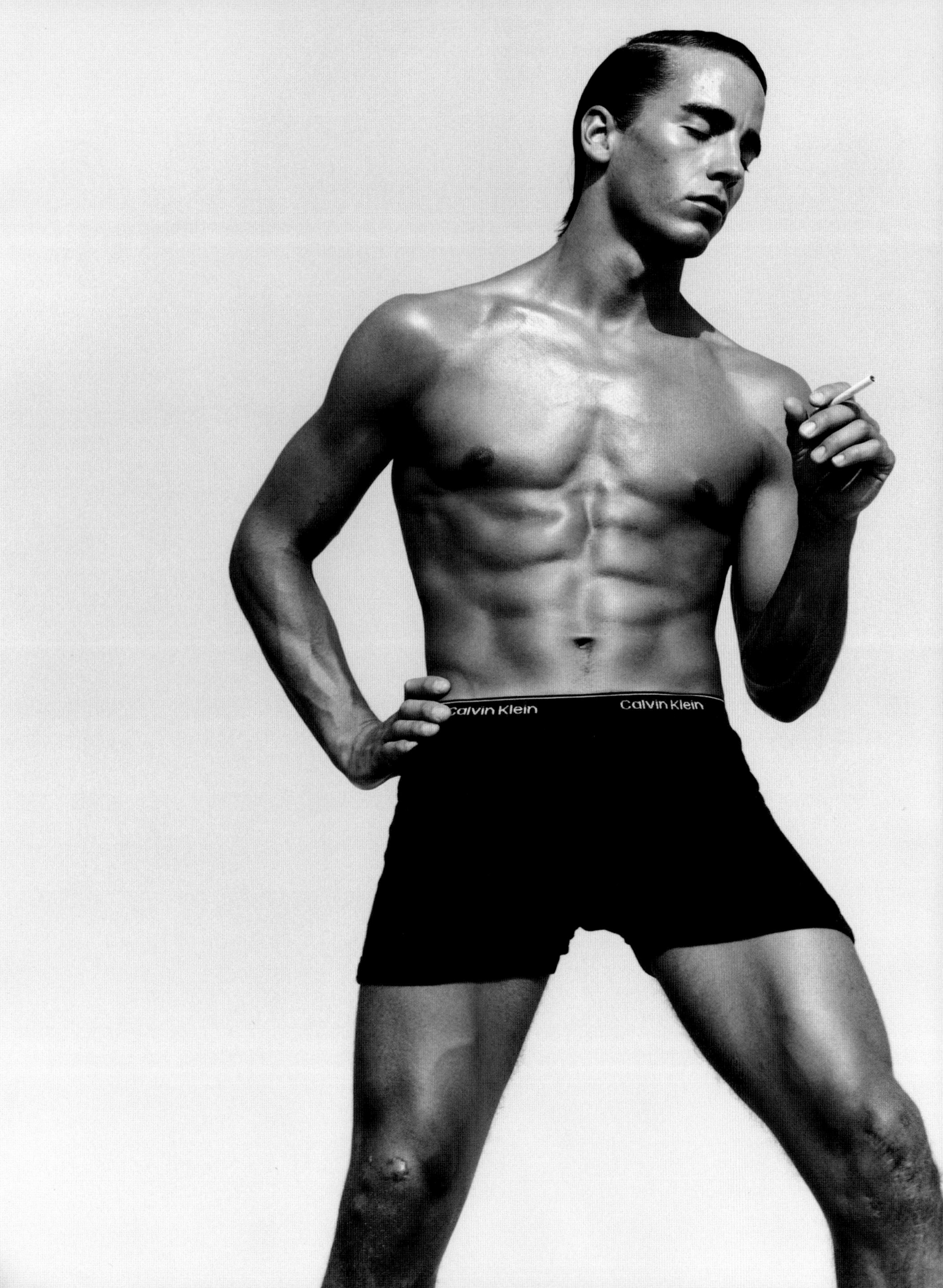

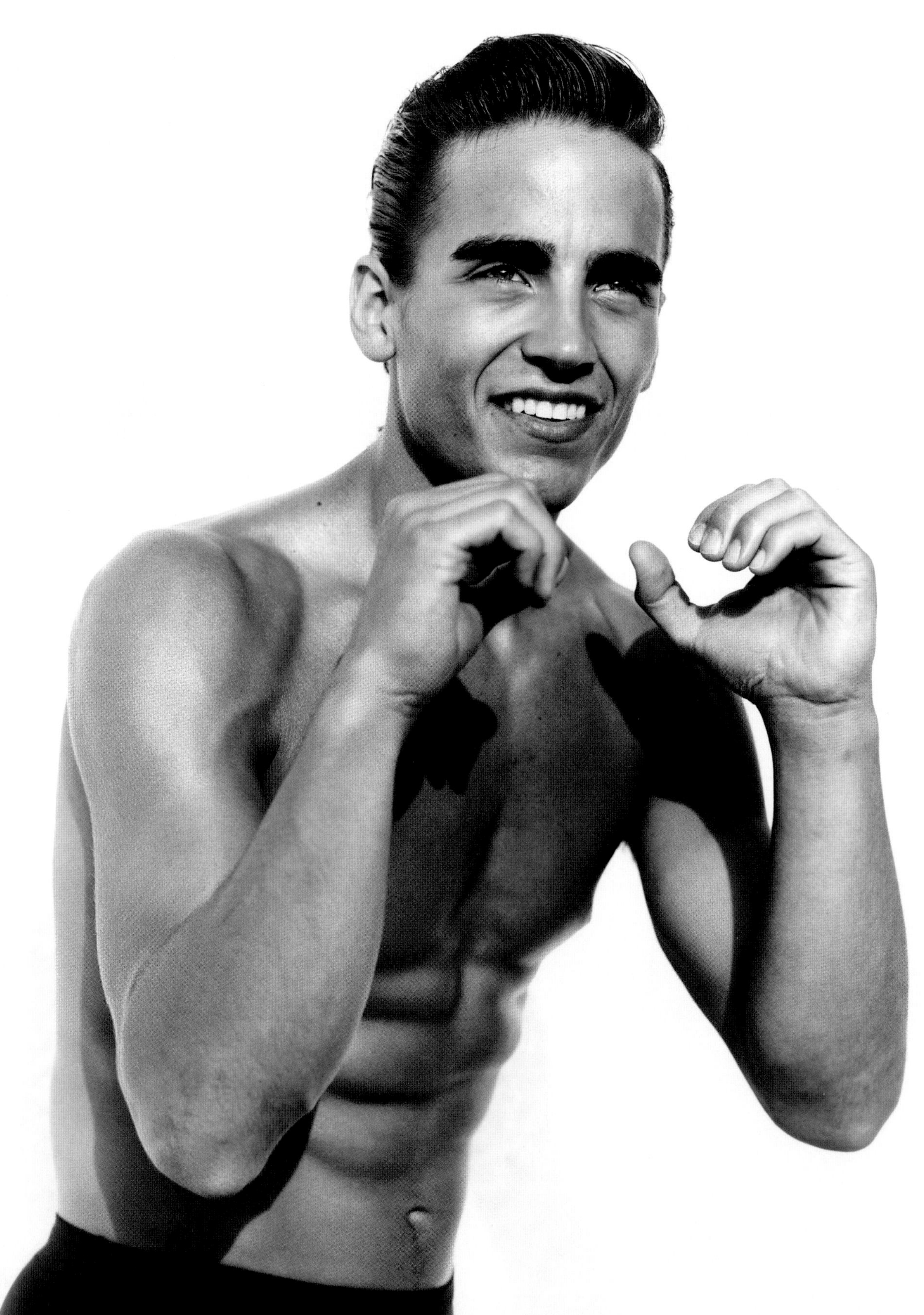

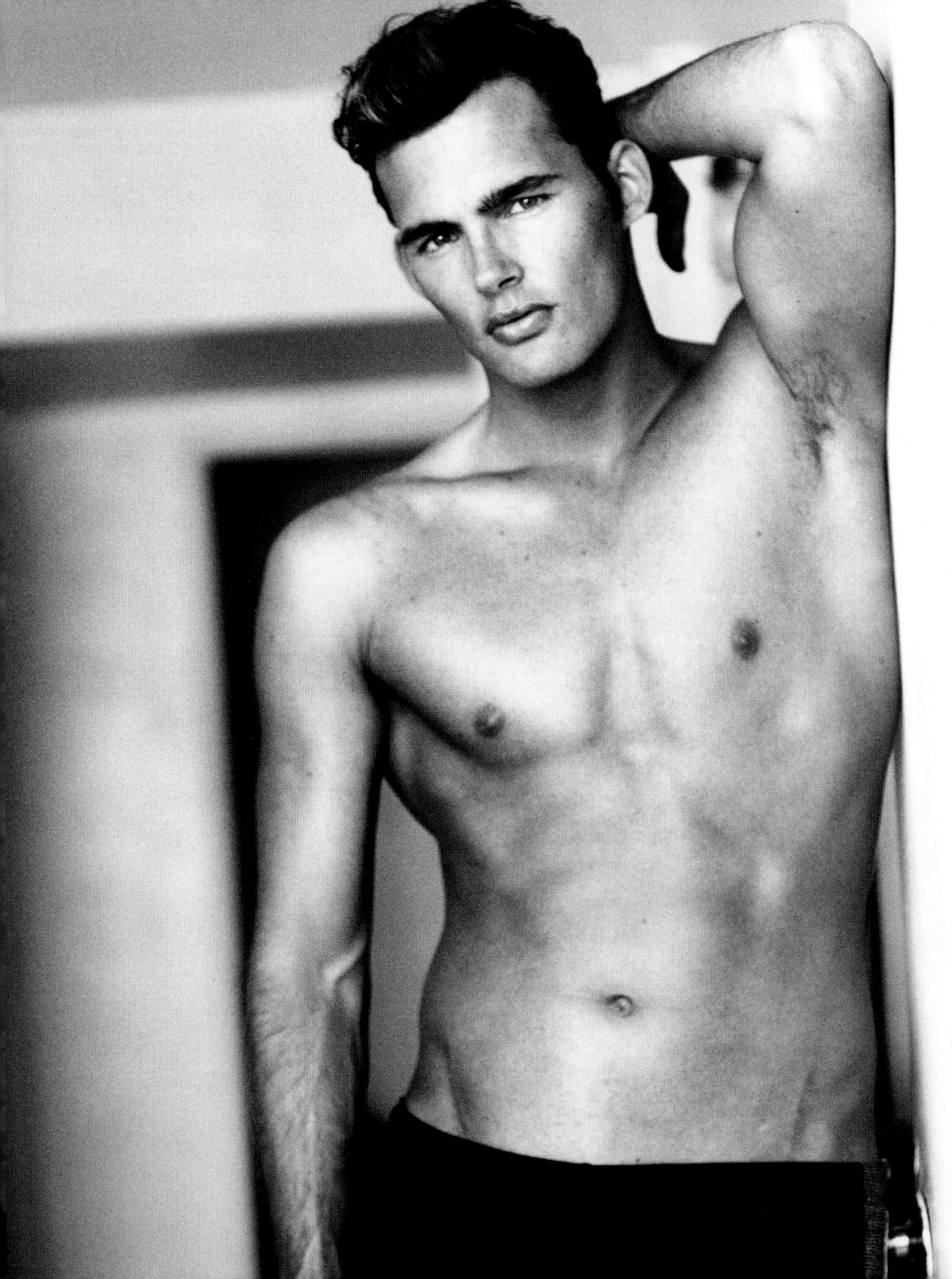

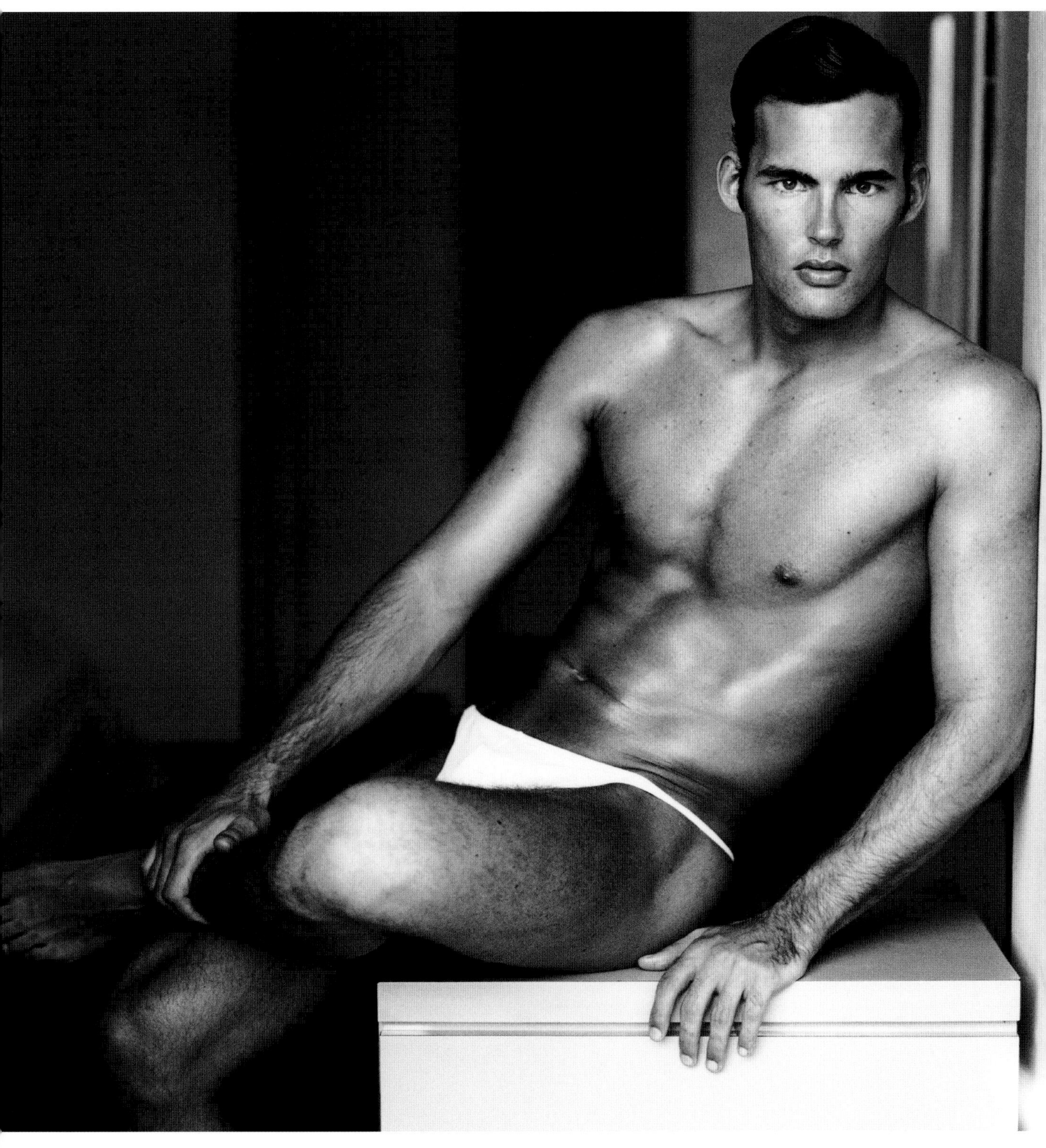

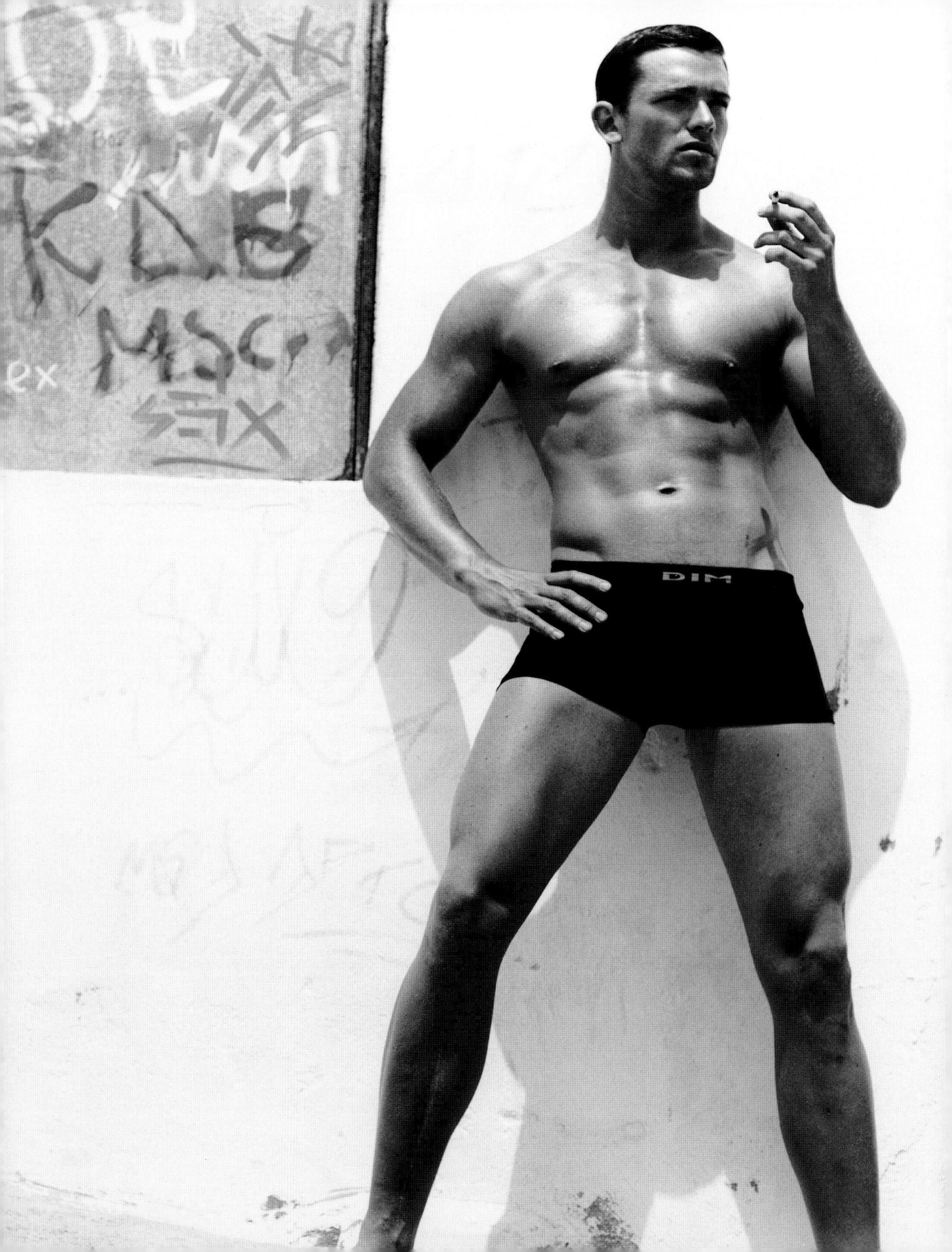
DIM

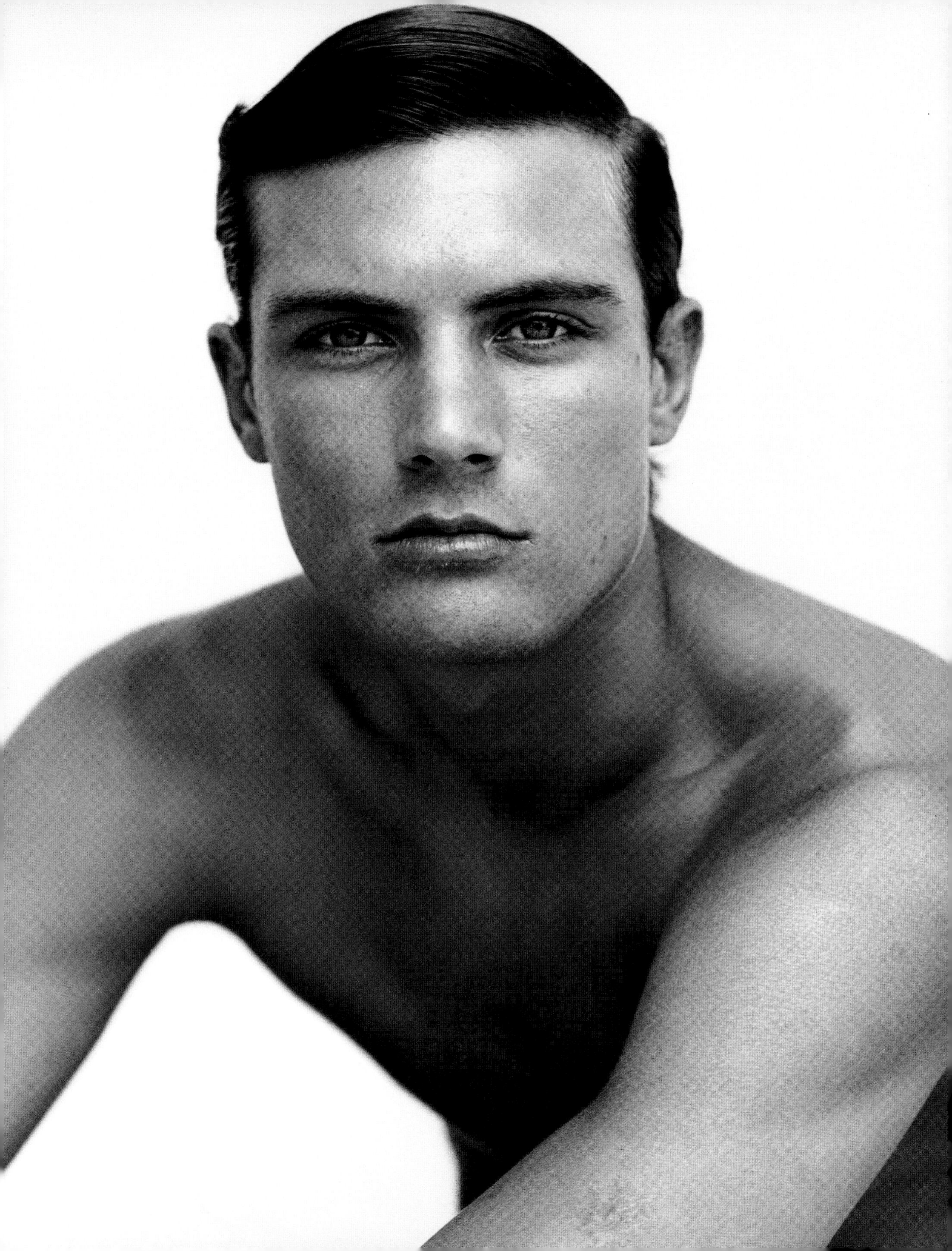

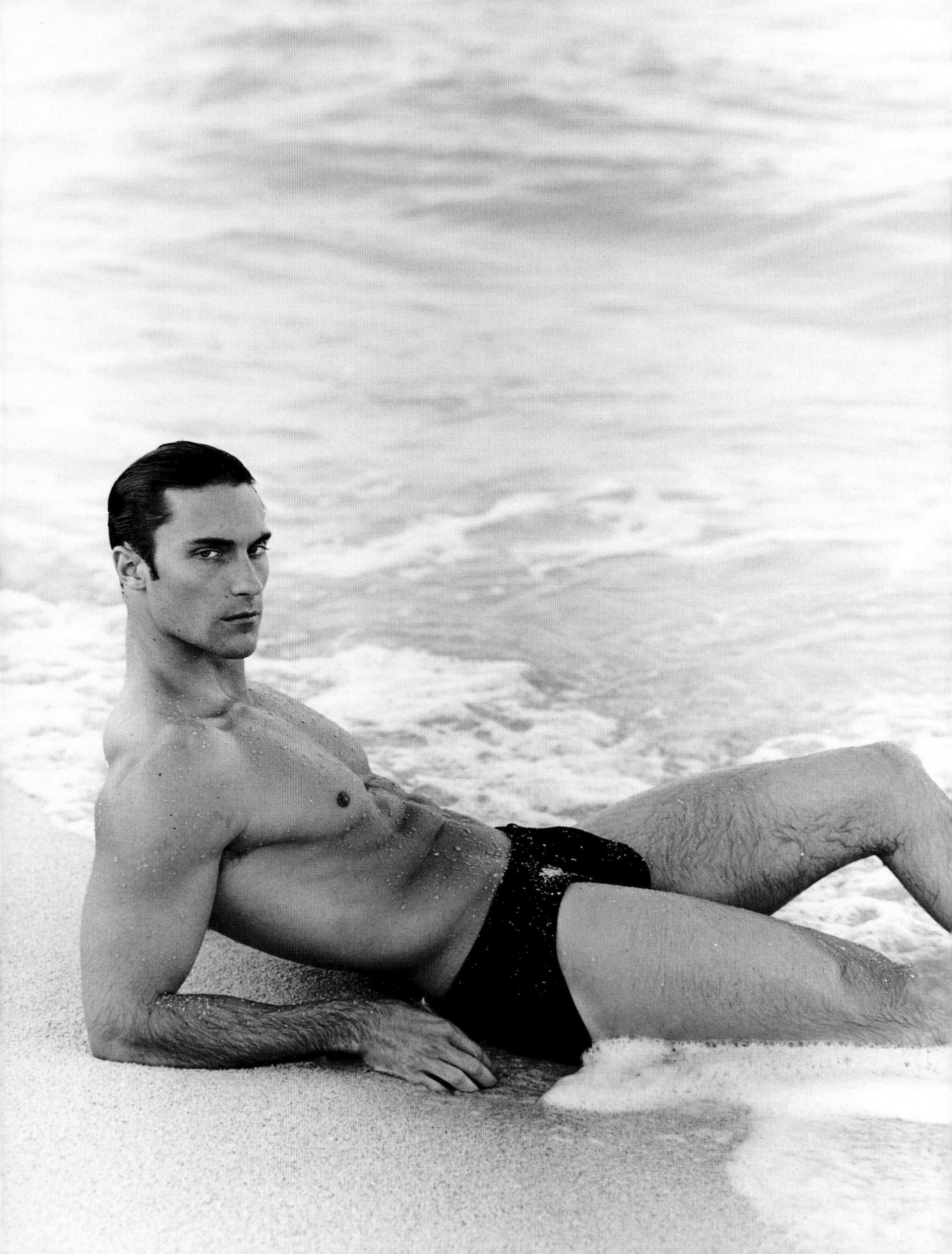

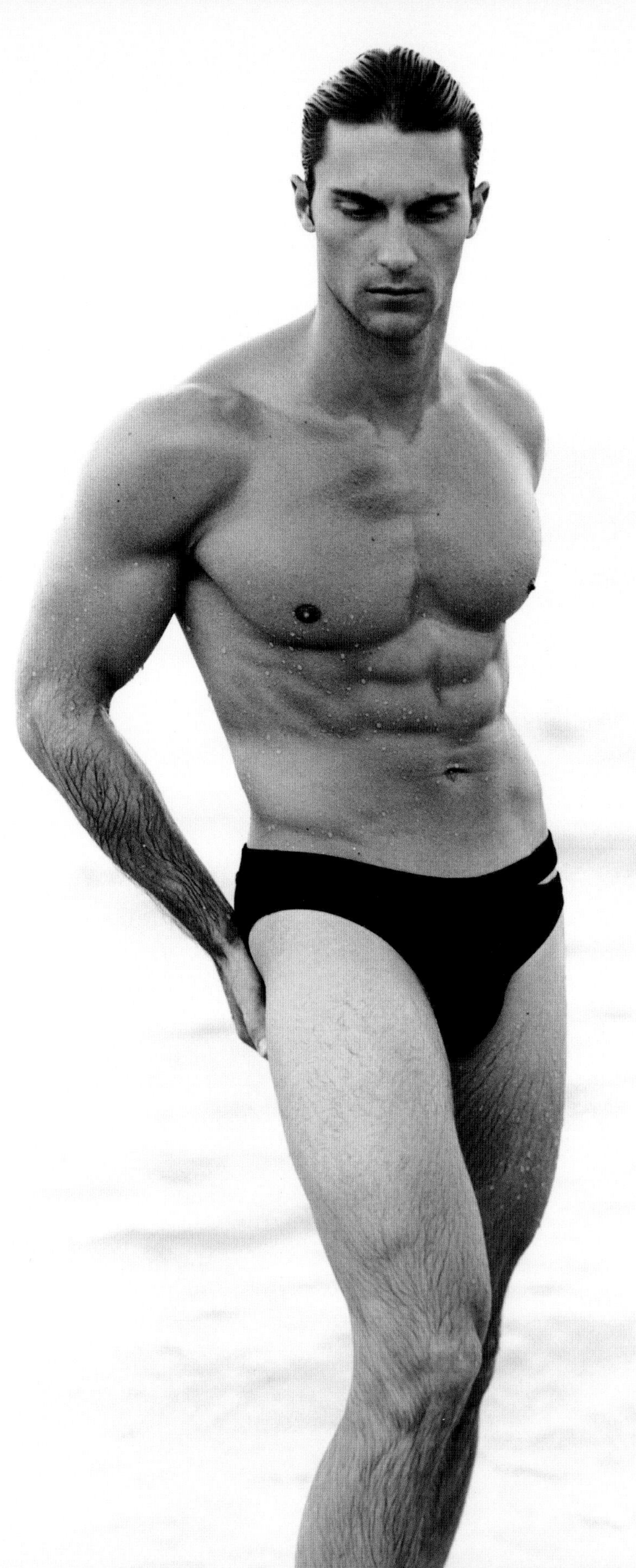

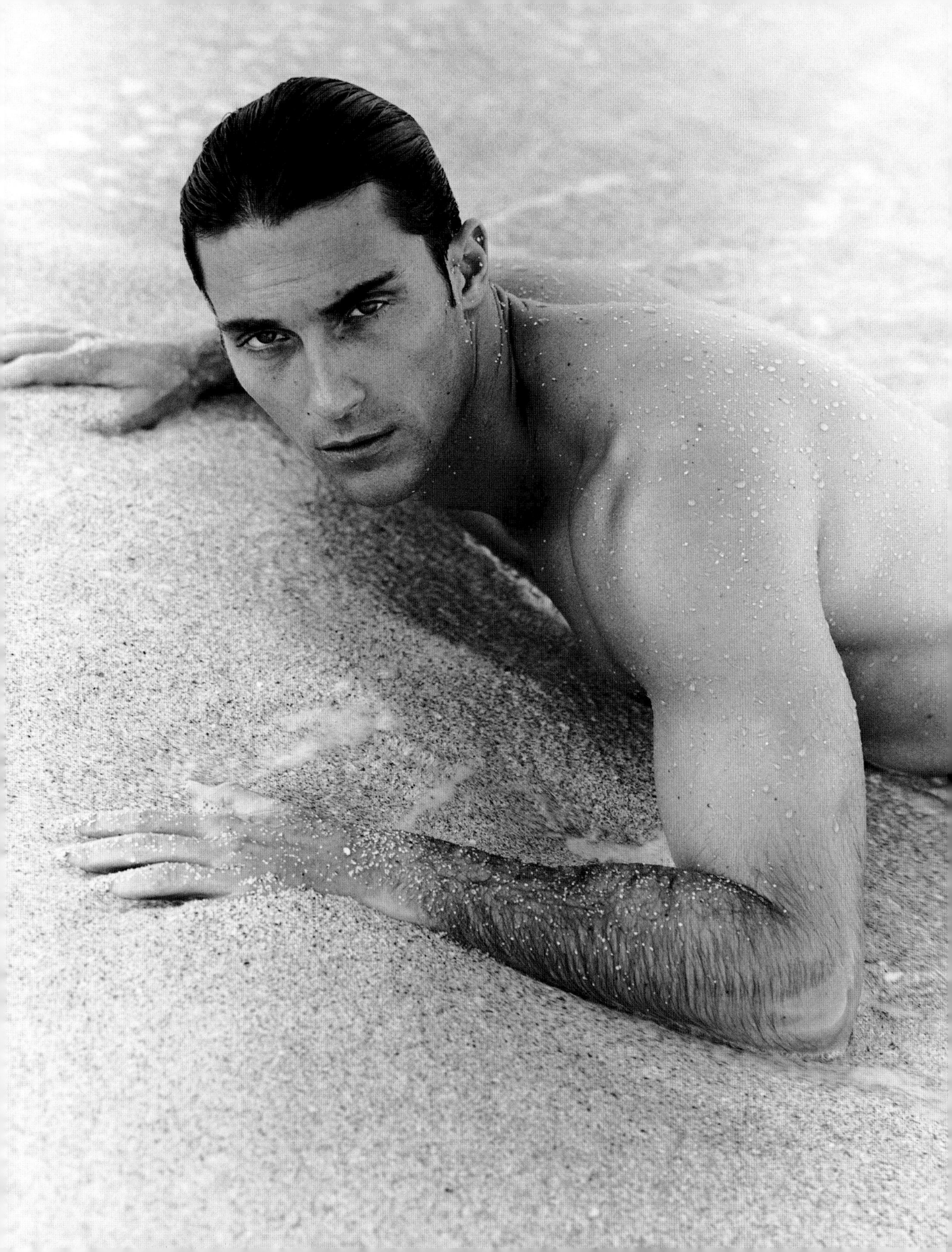

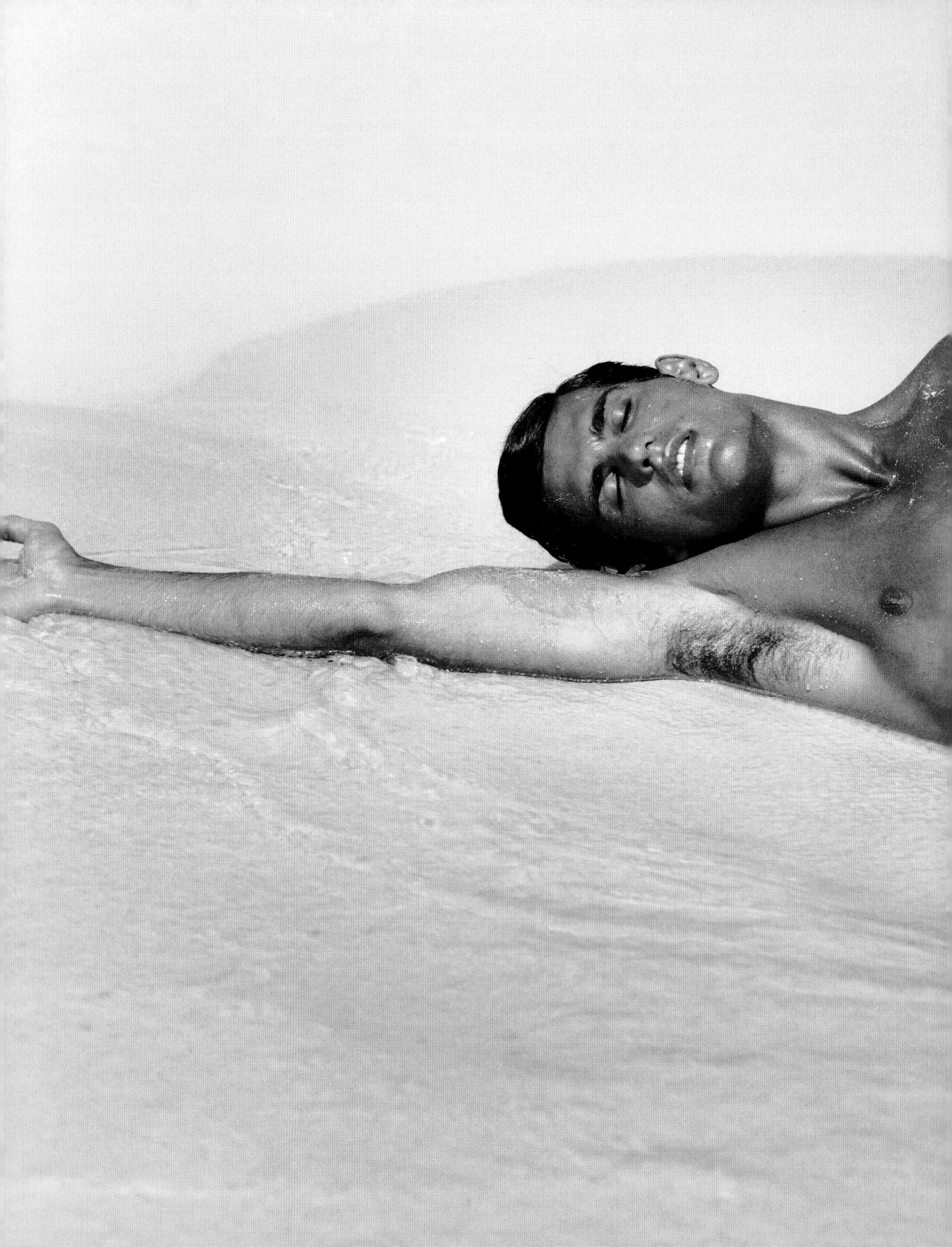

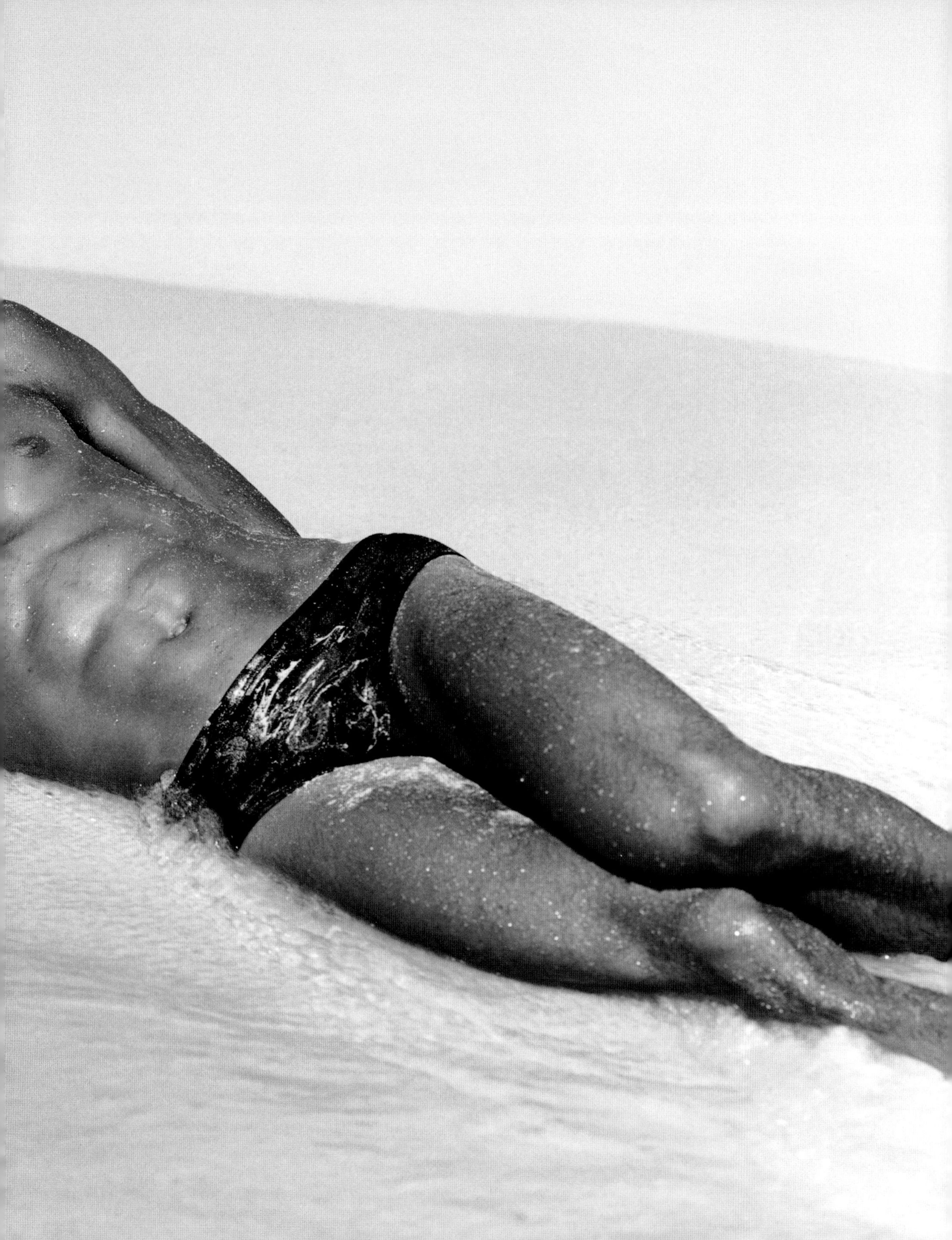

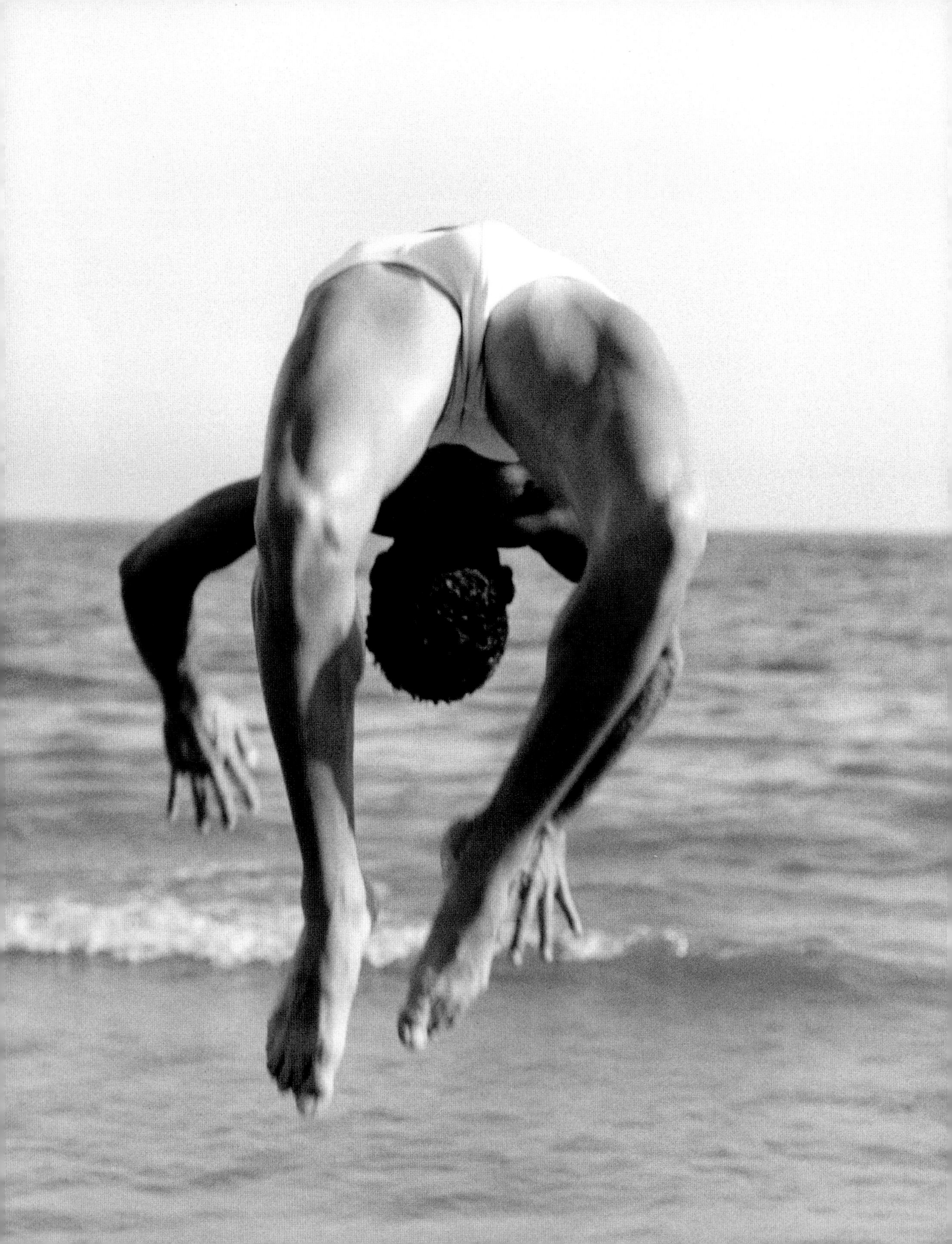

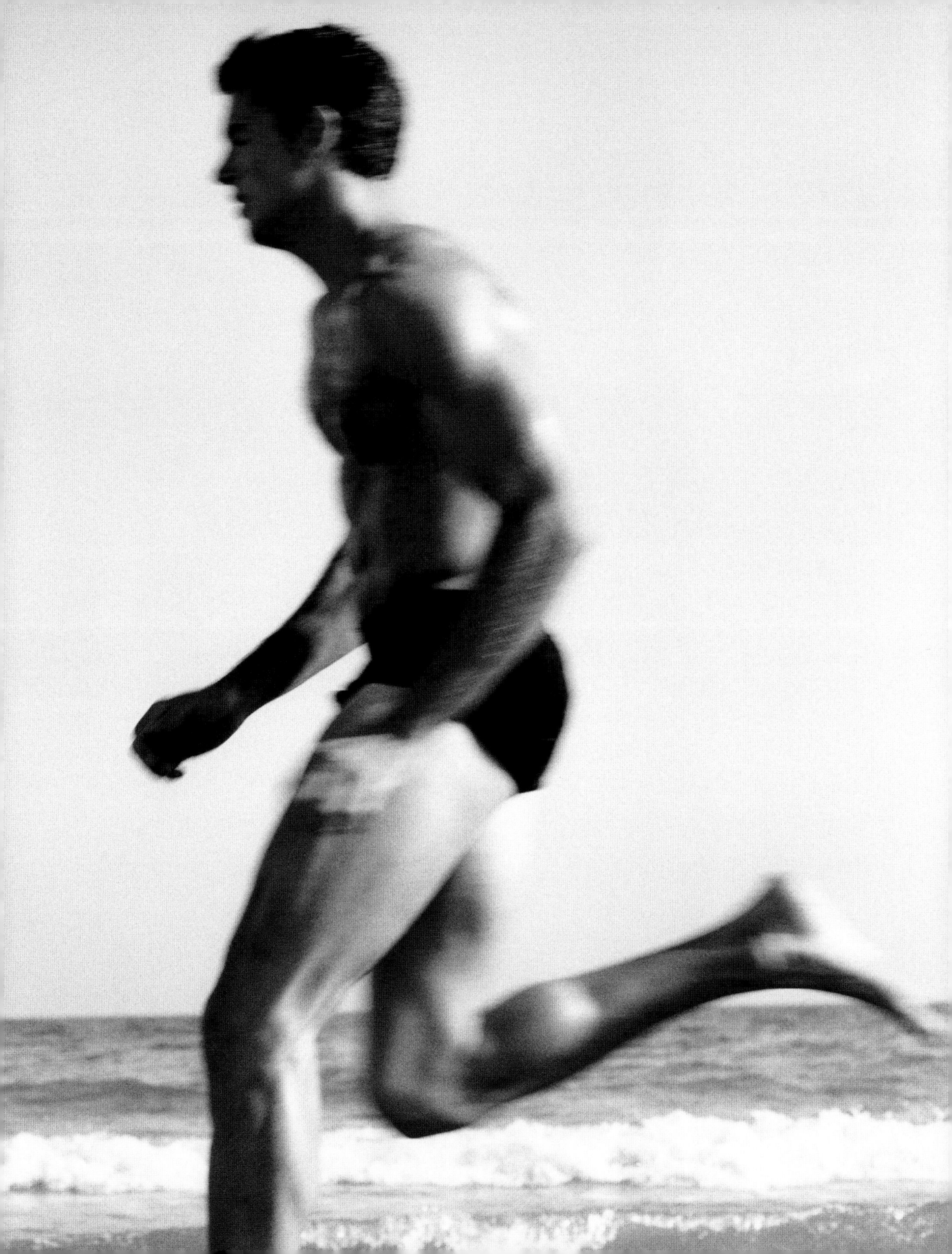

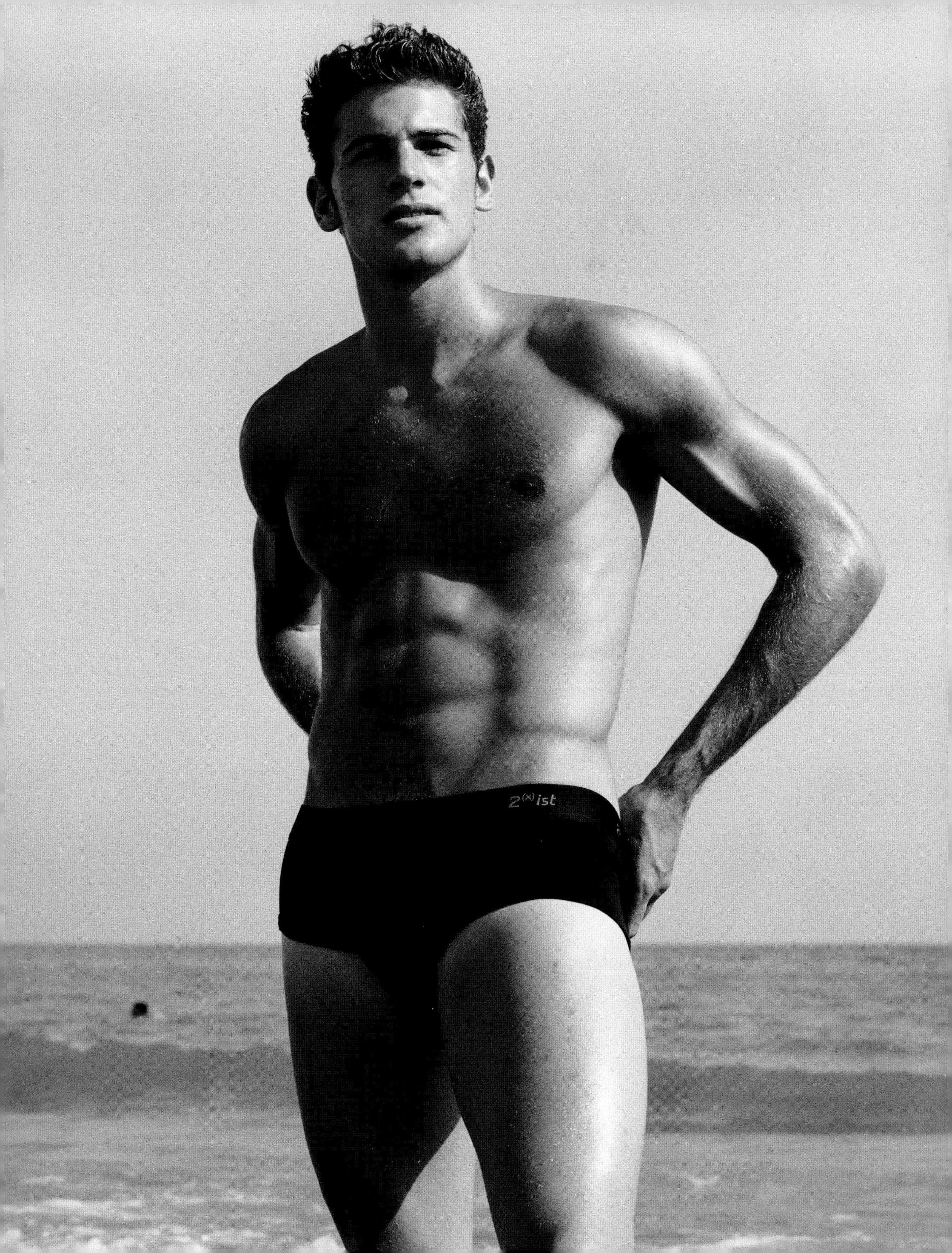

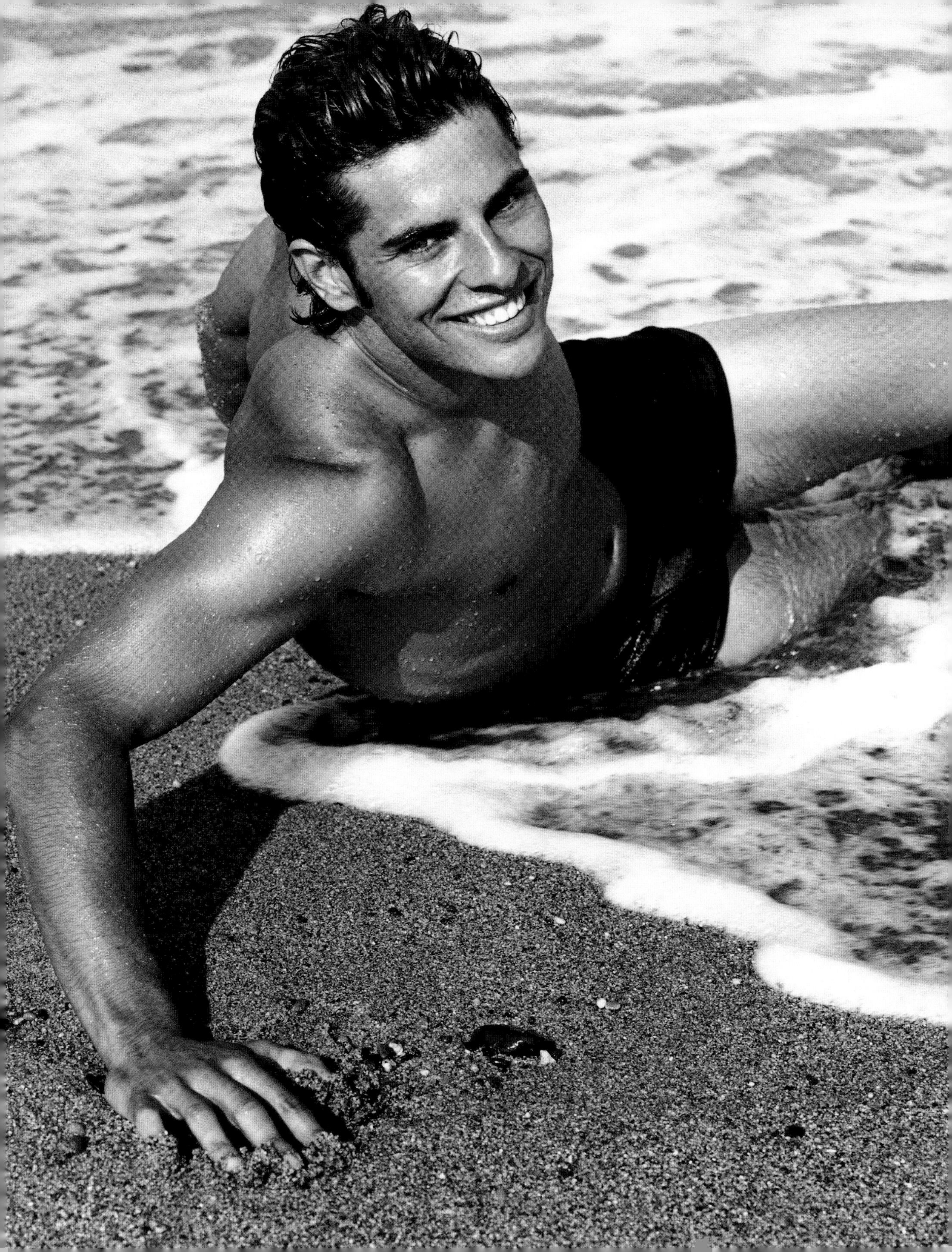

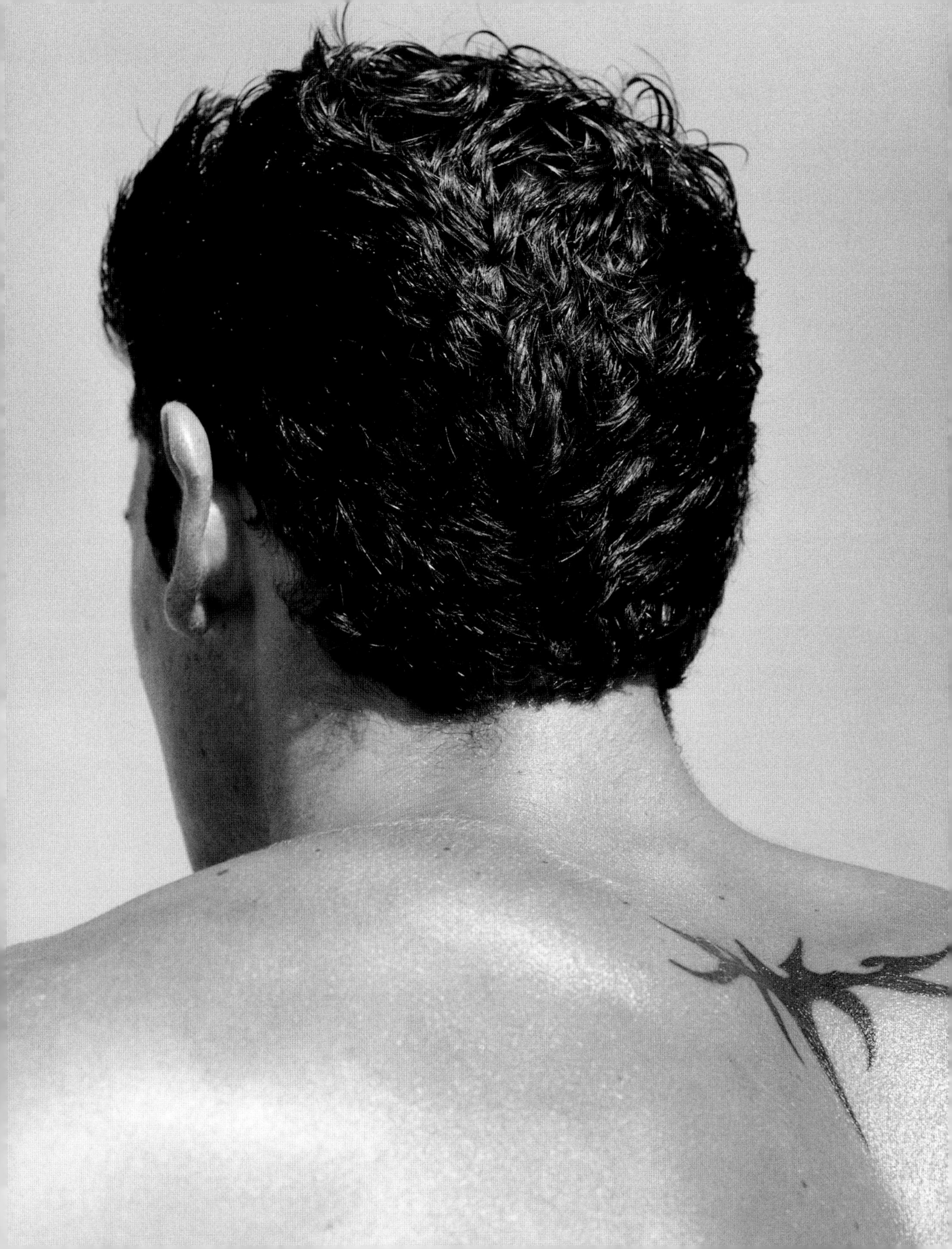

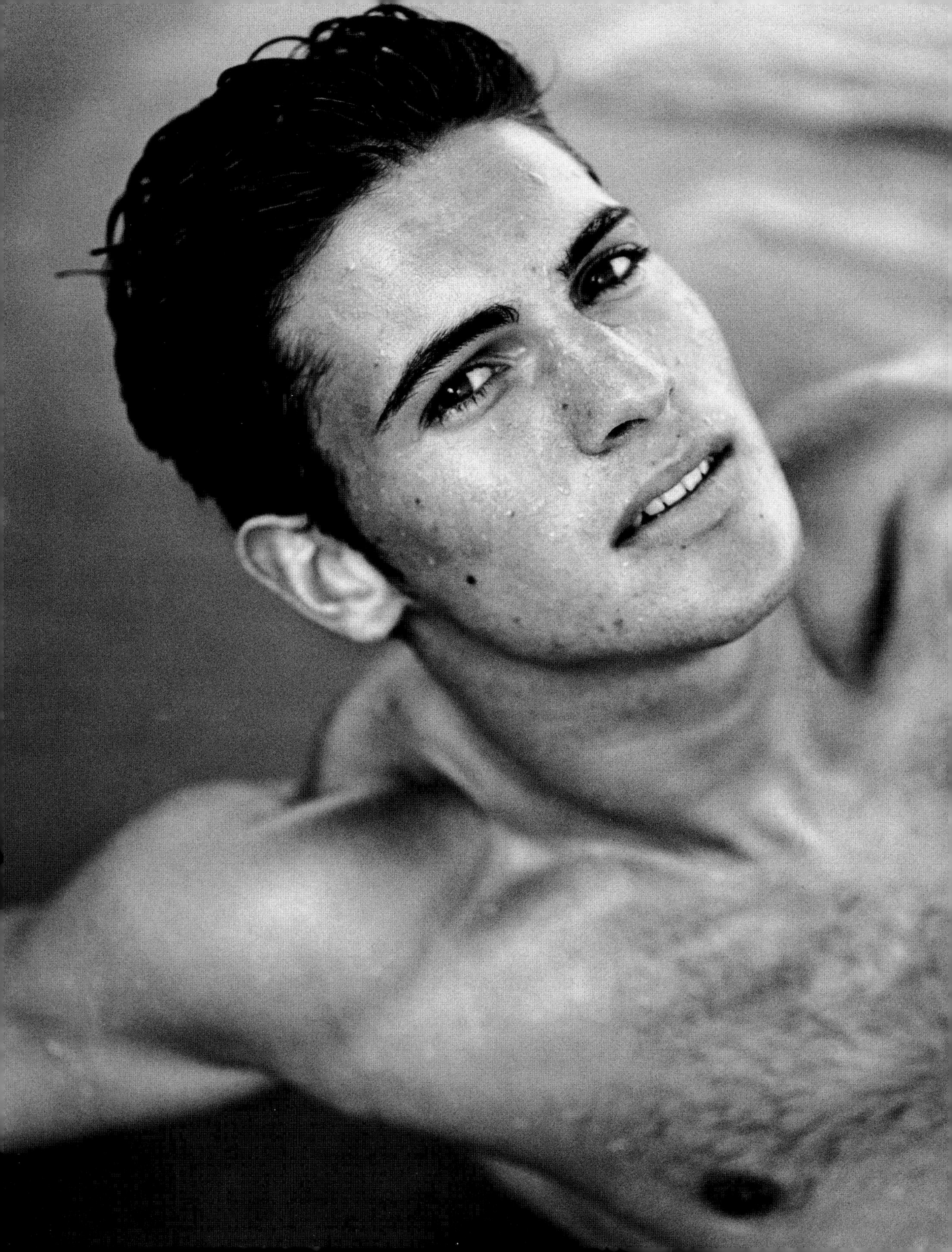

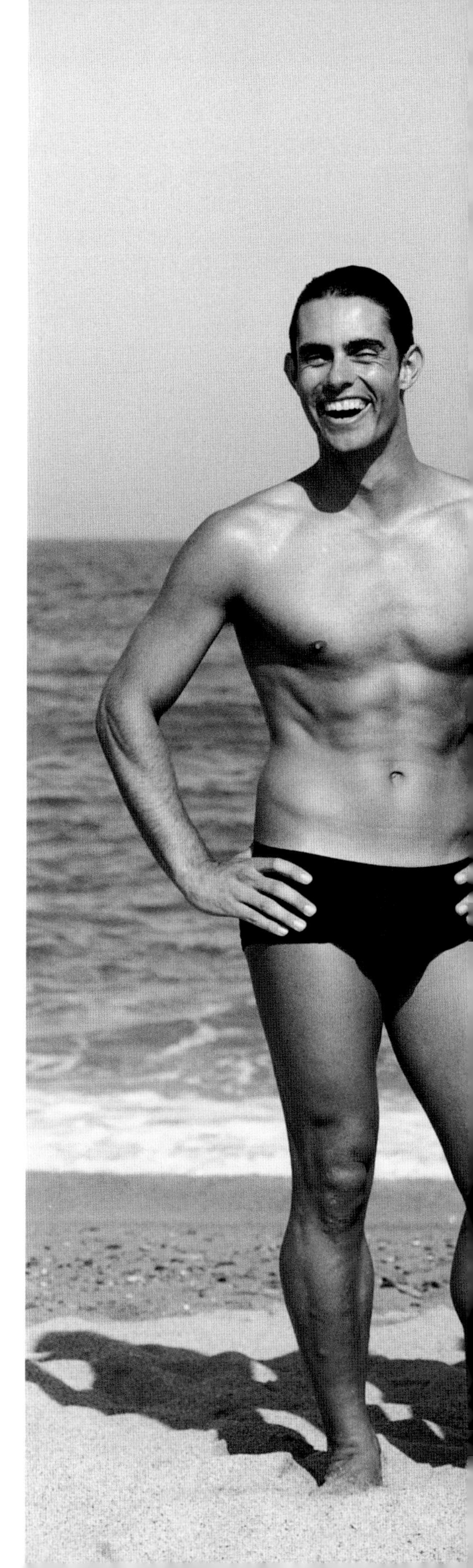

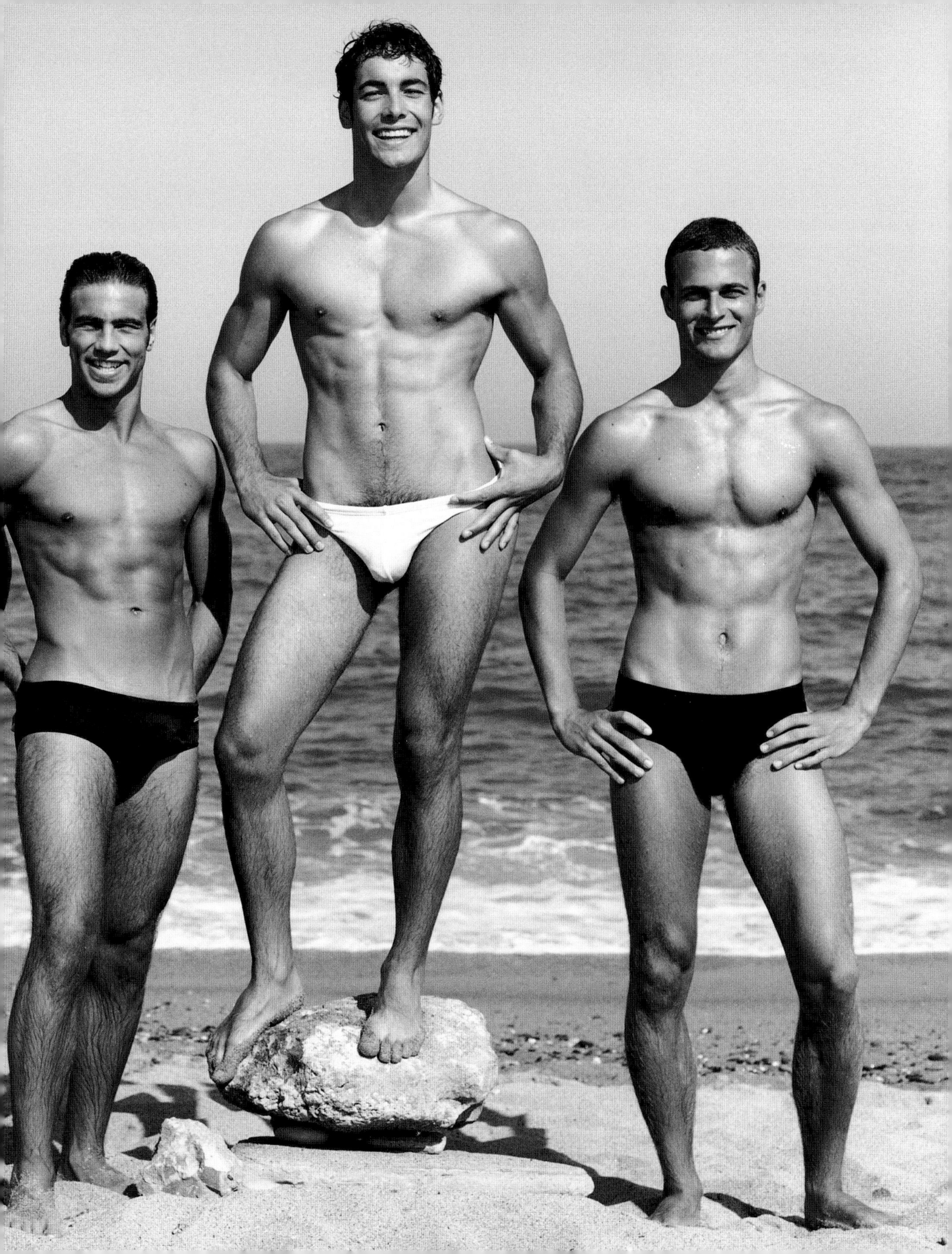

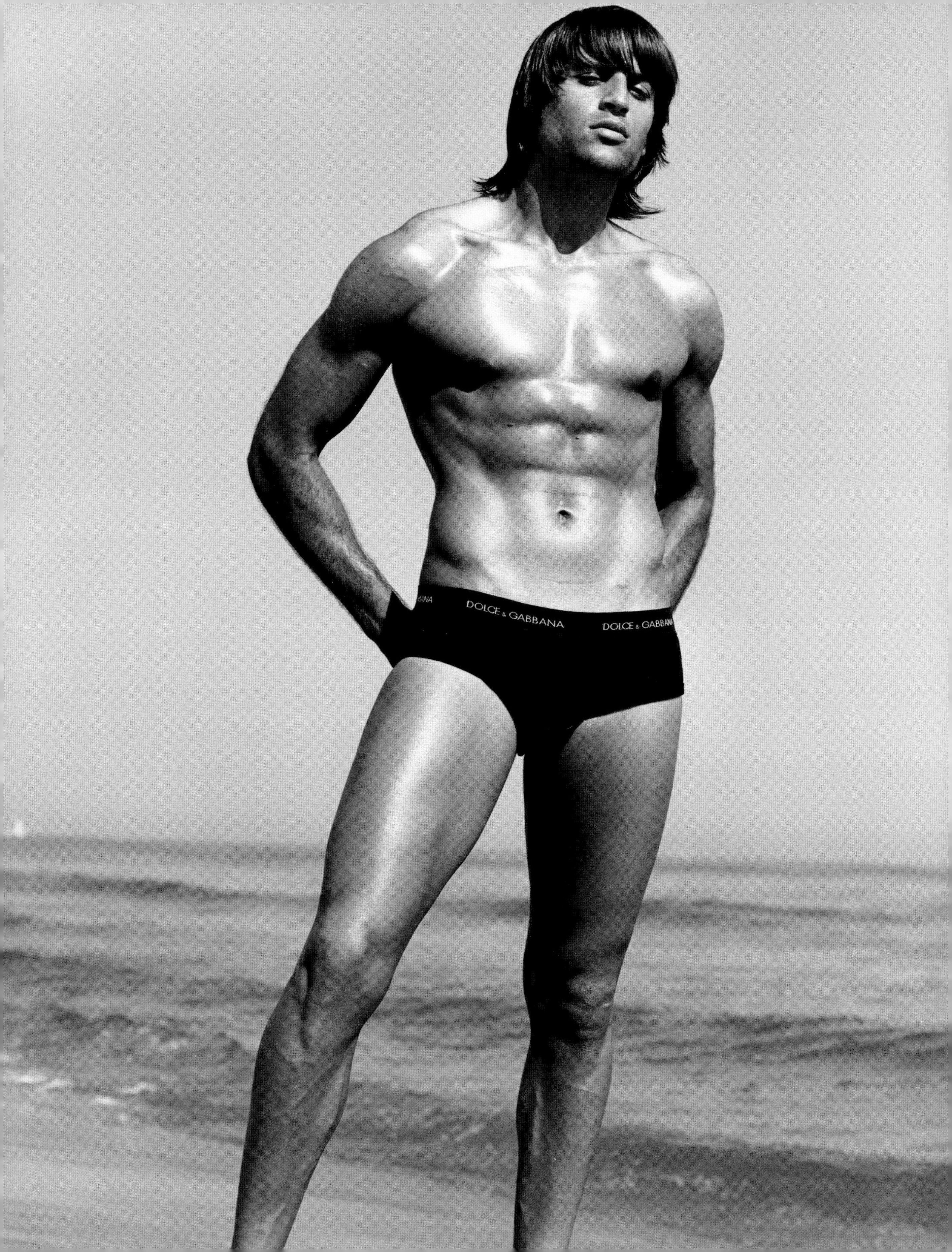

DOLCE & GABBANA
DOLCE & GABBANA

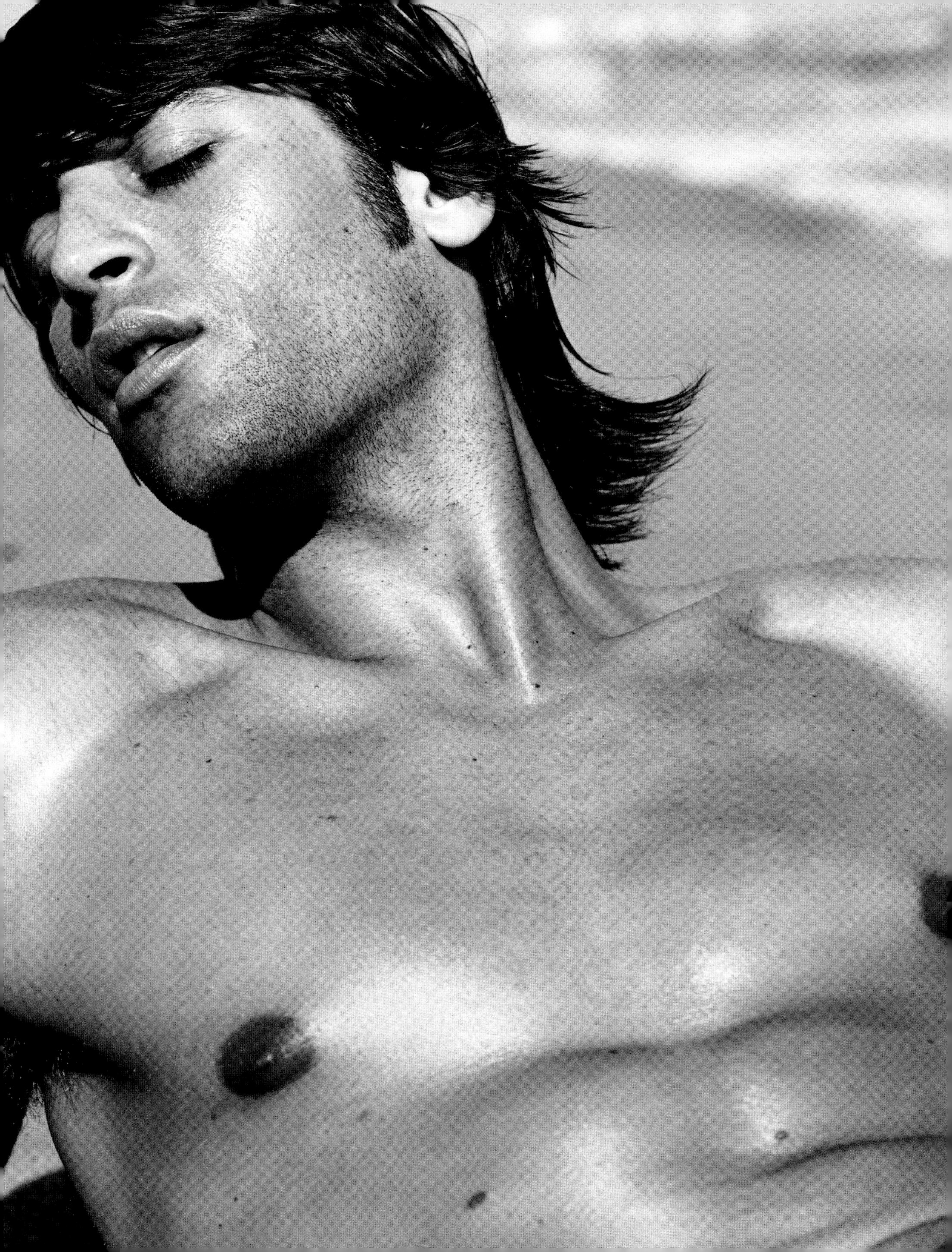

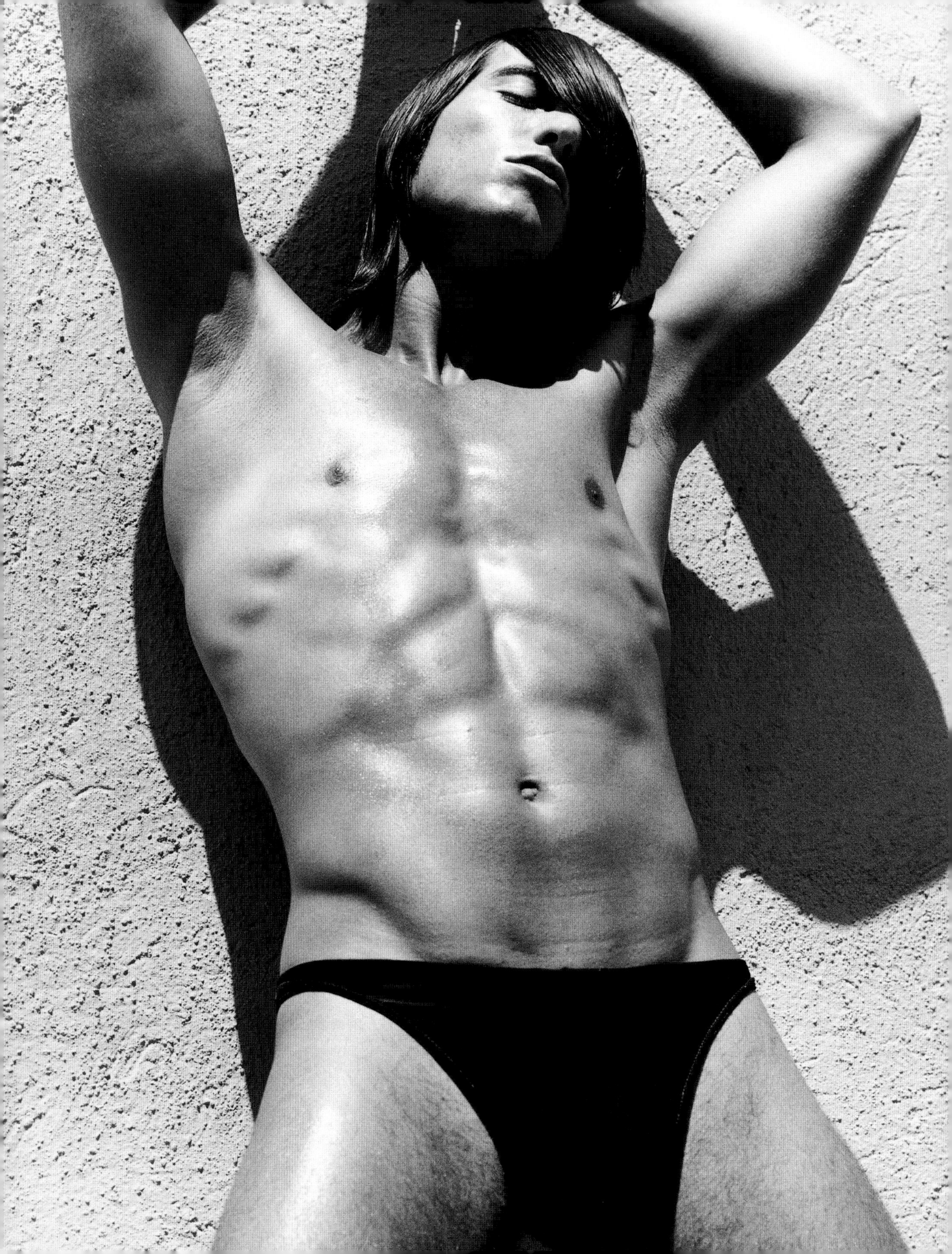

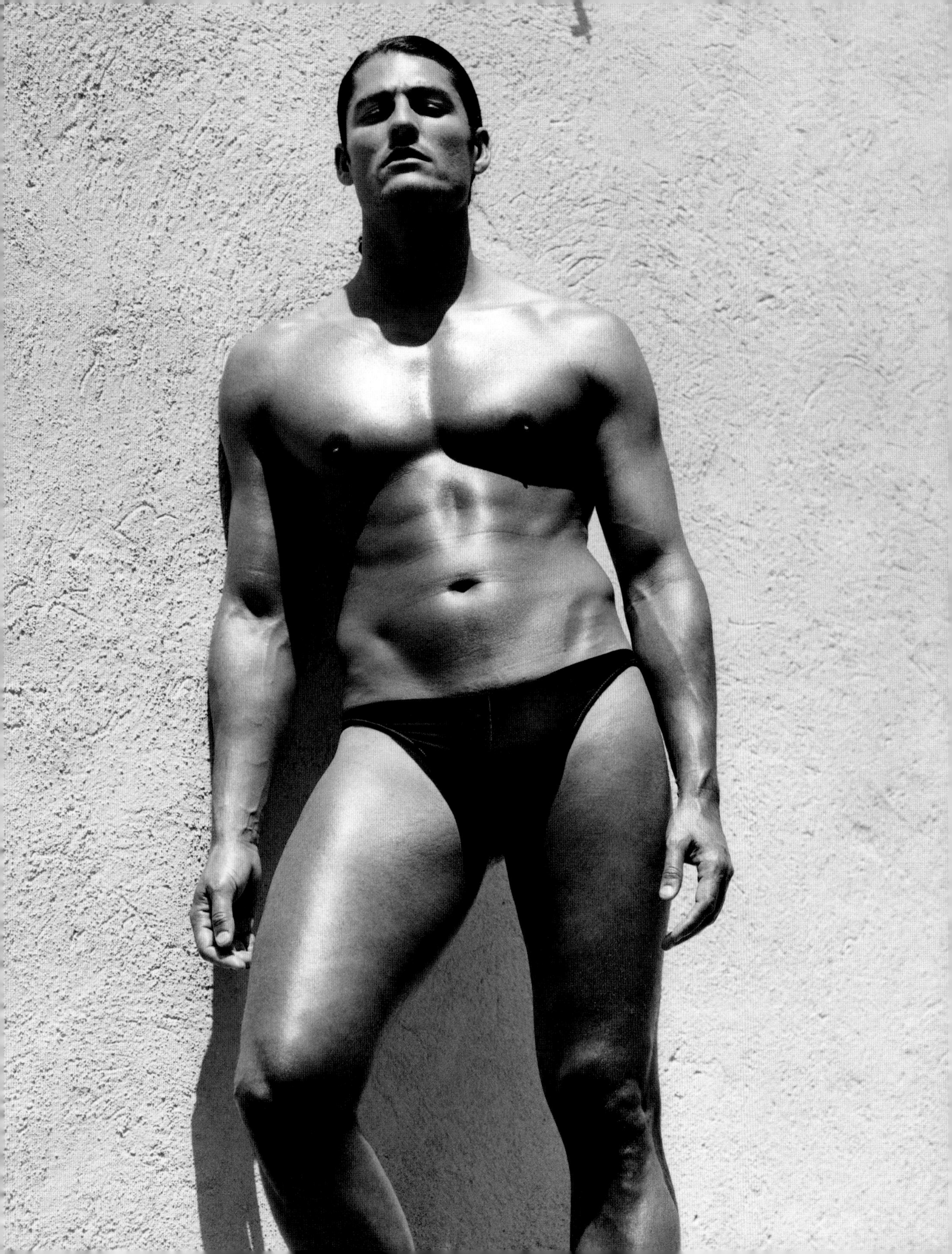

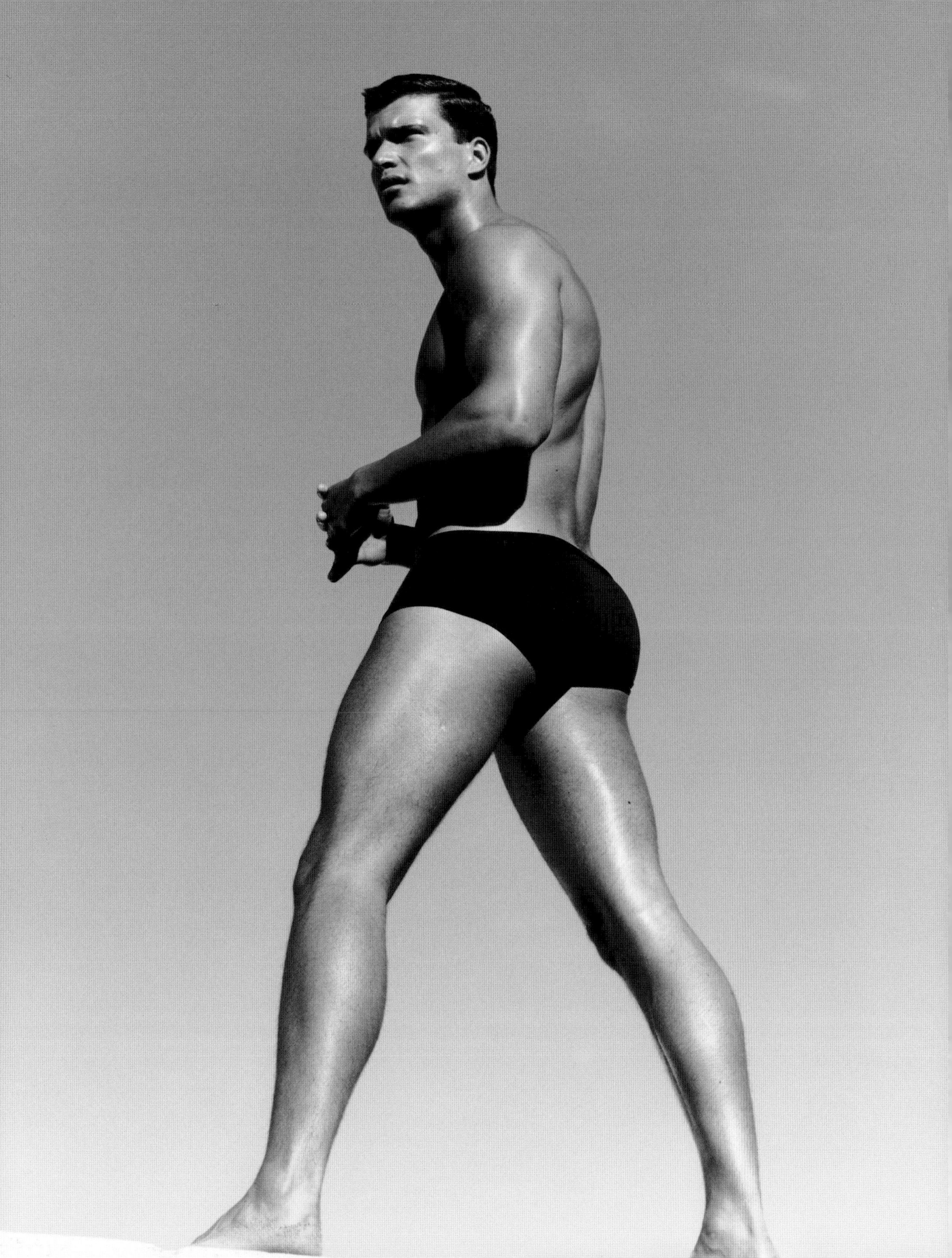

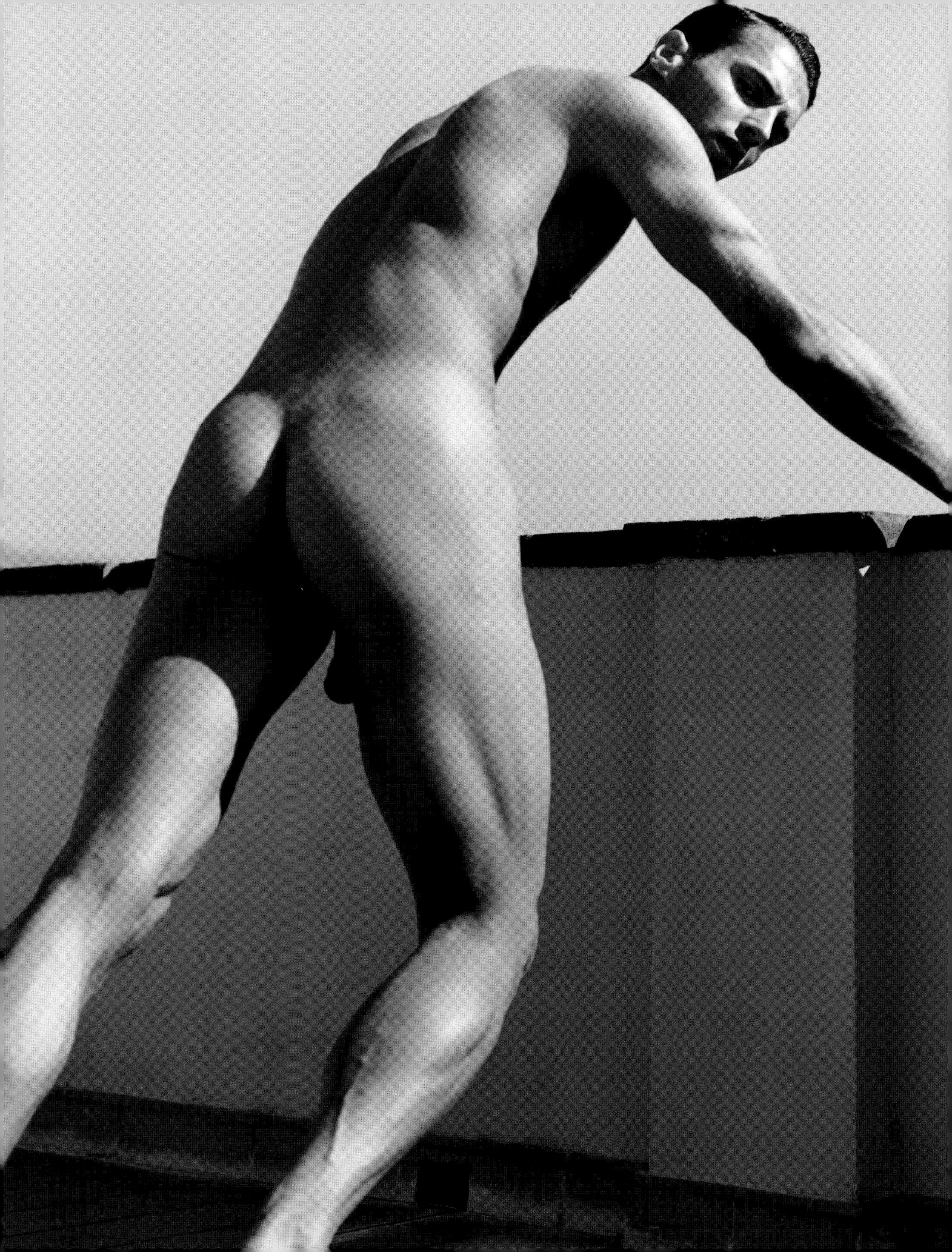

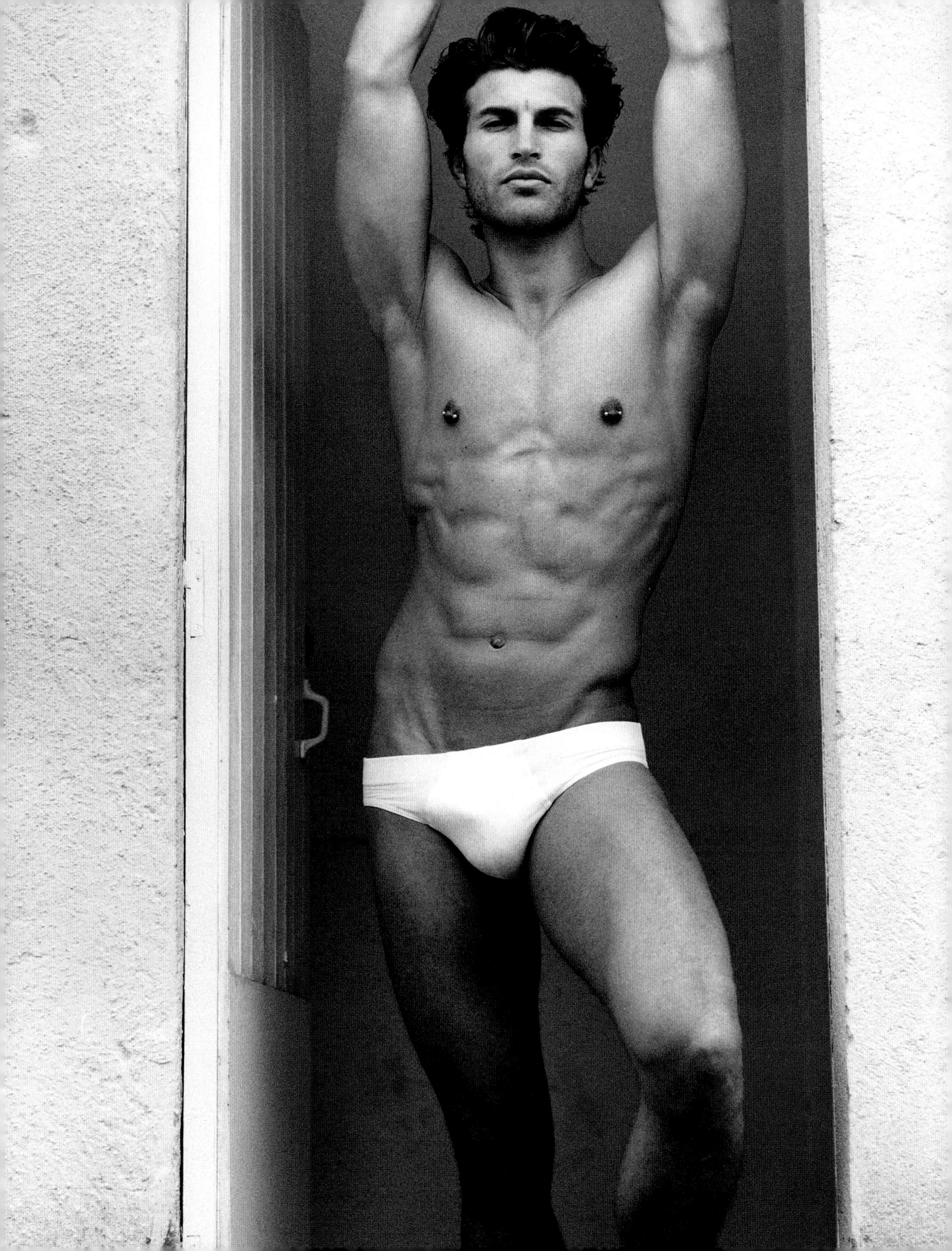

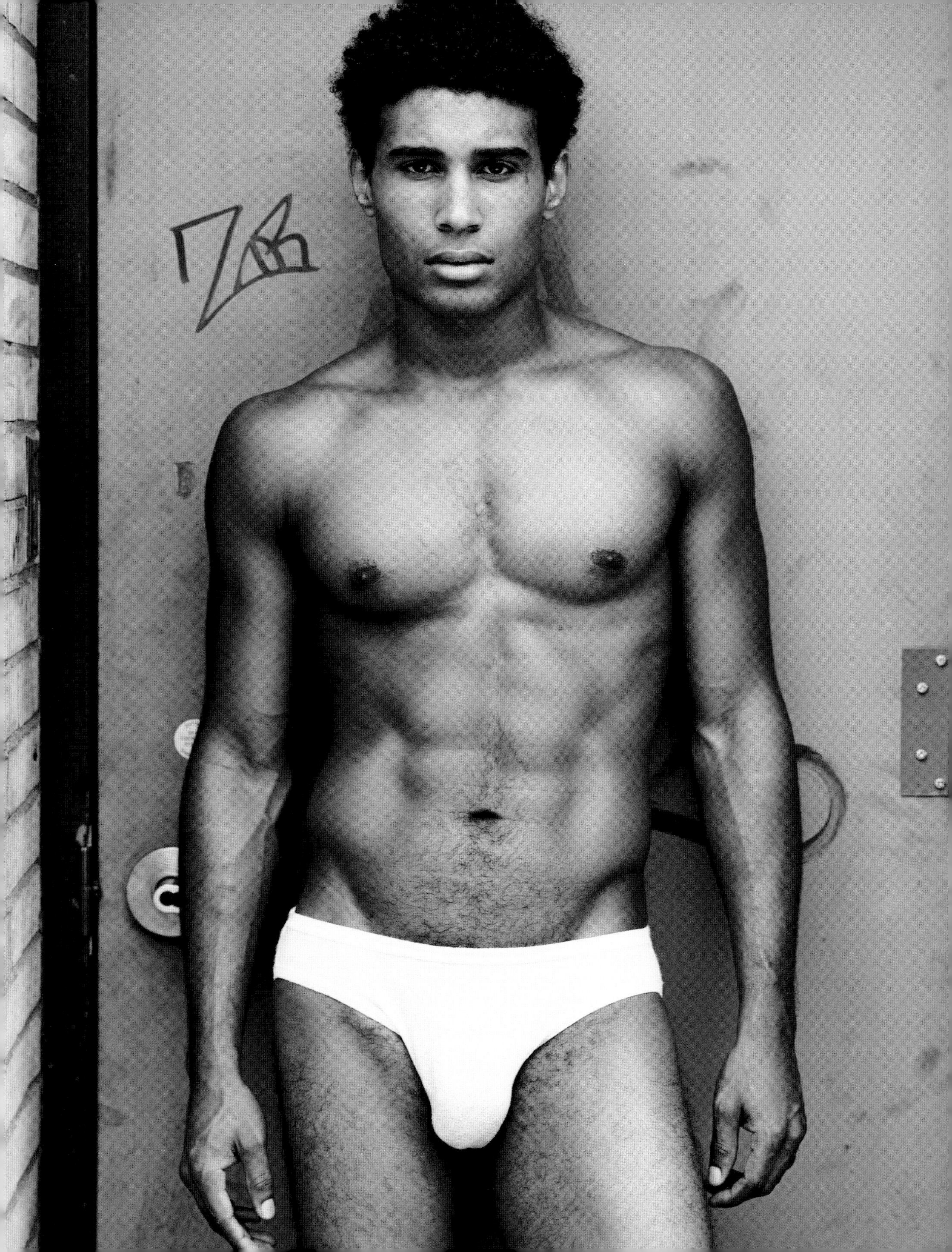

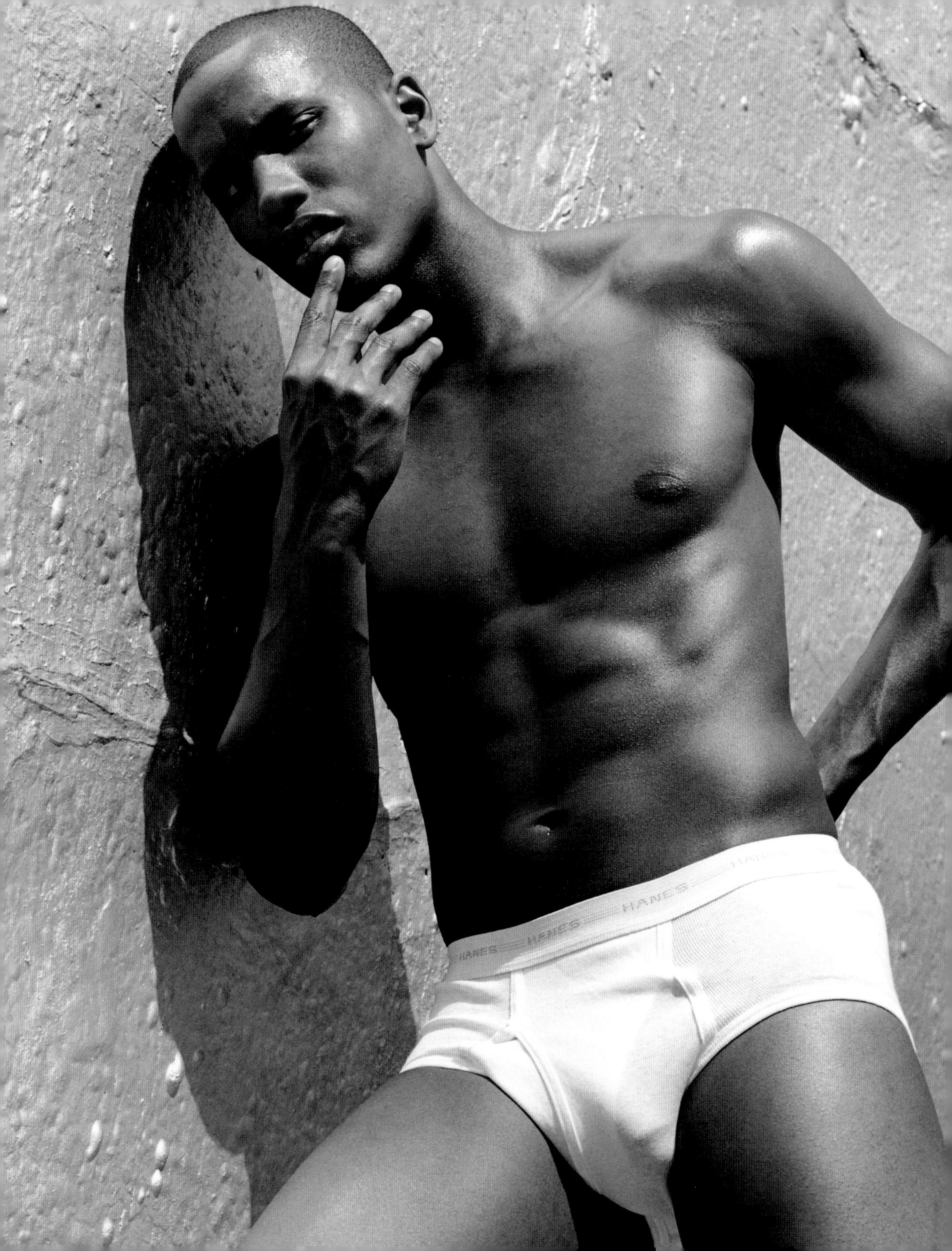

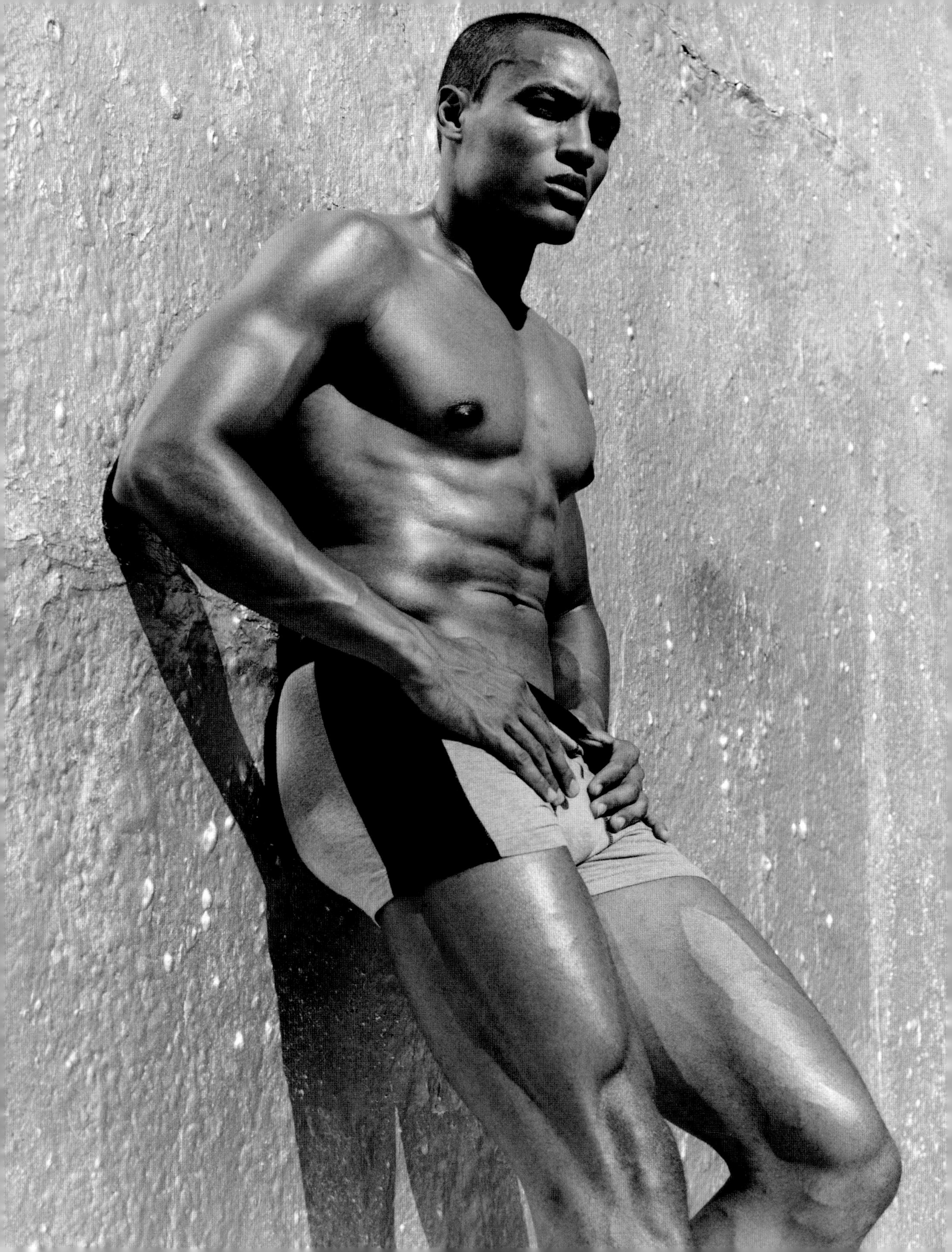

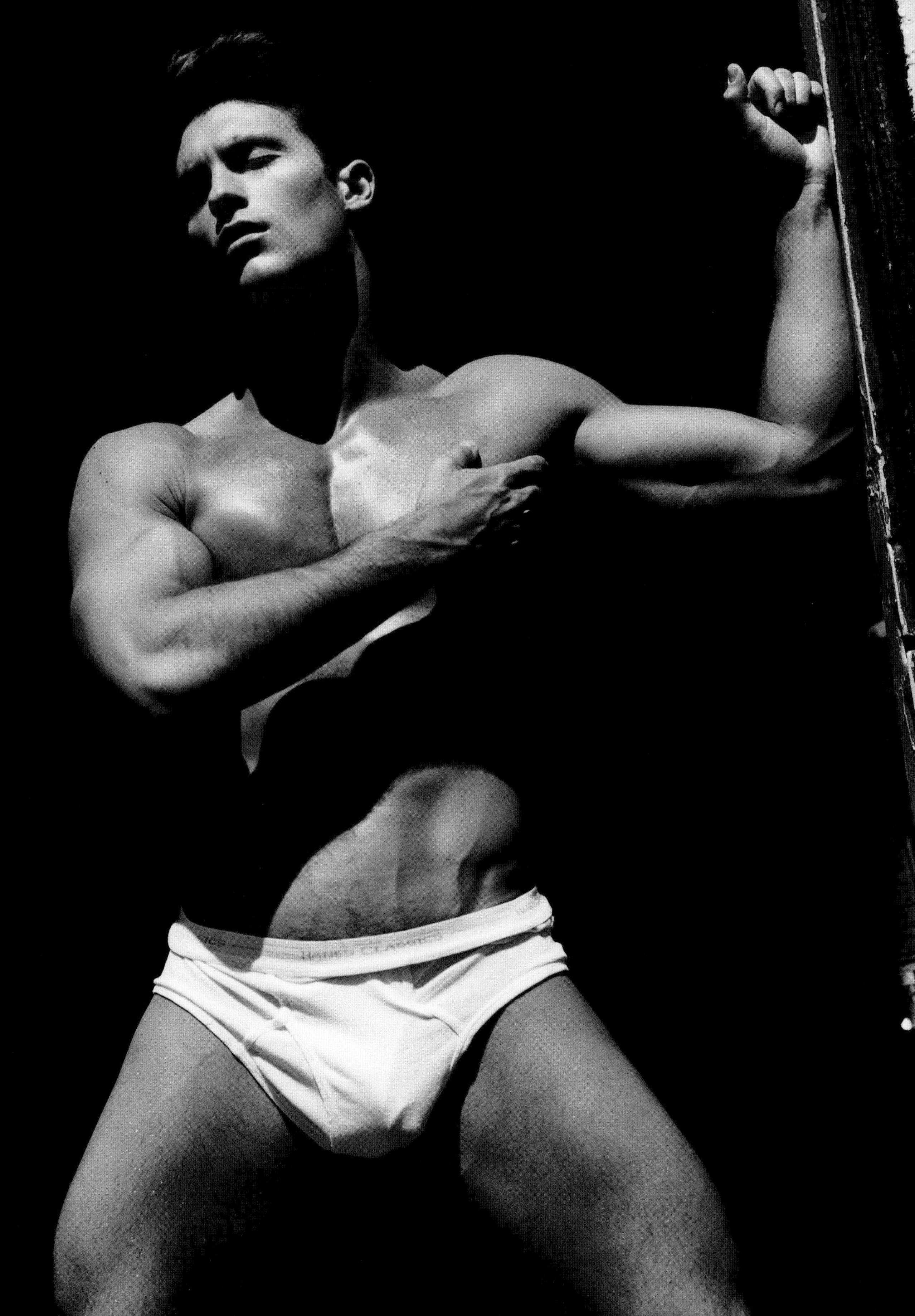

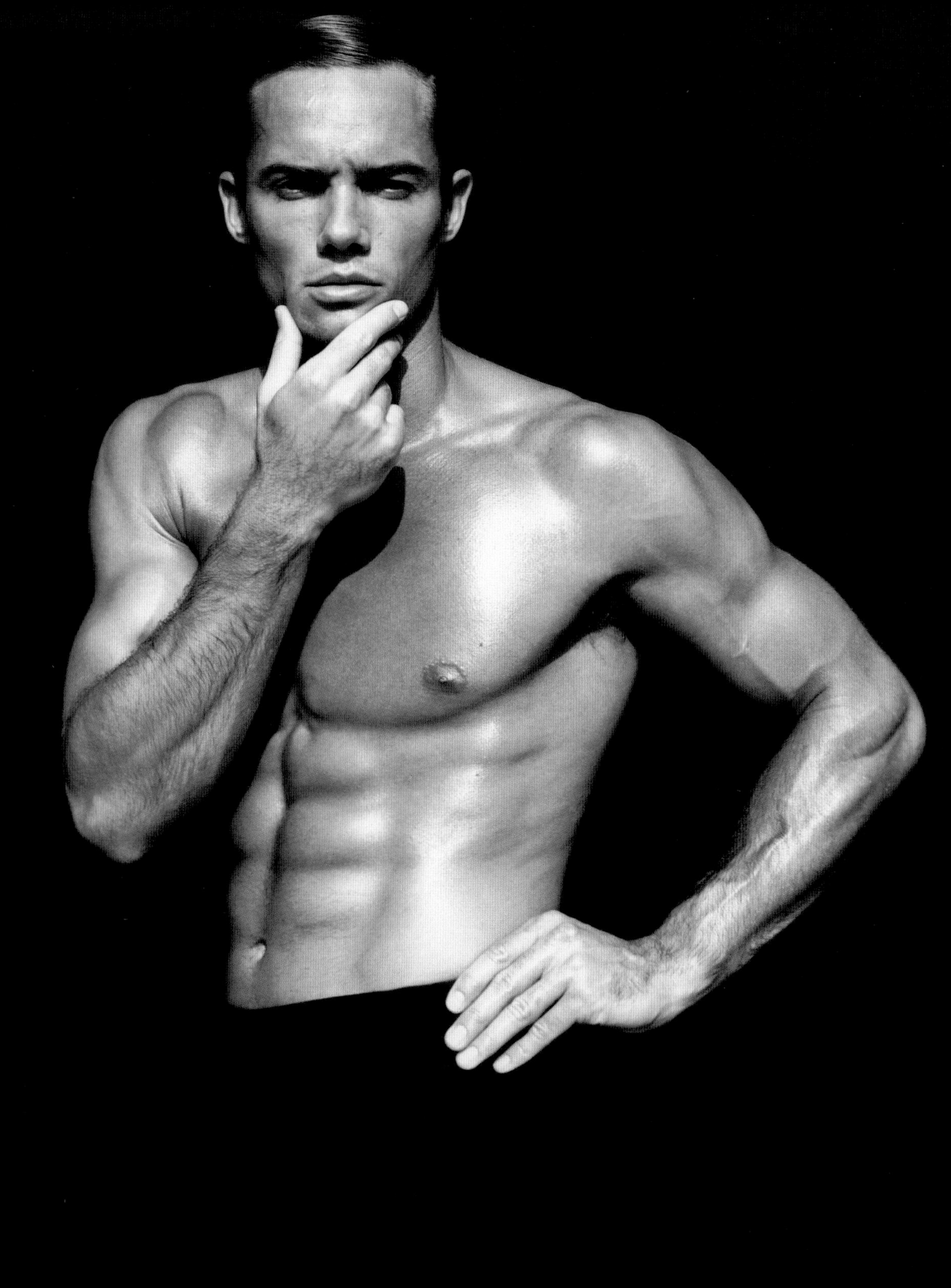

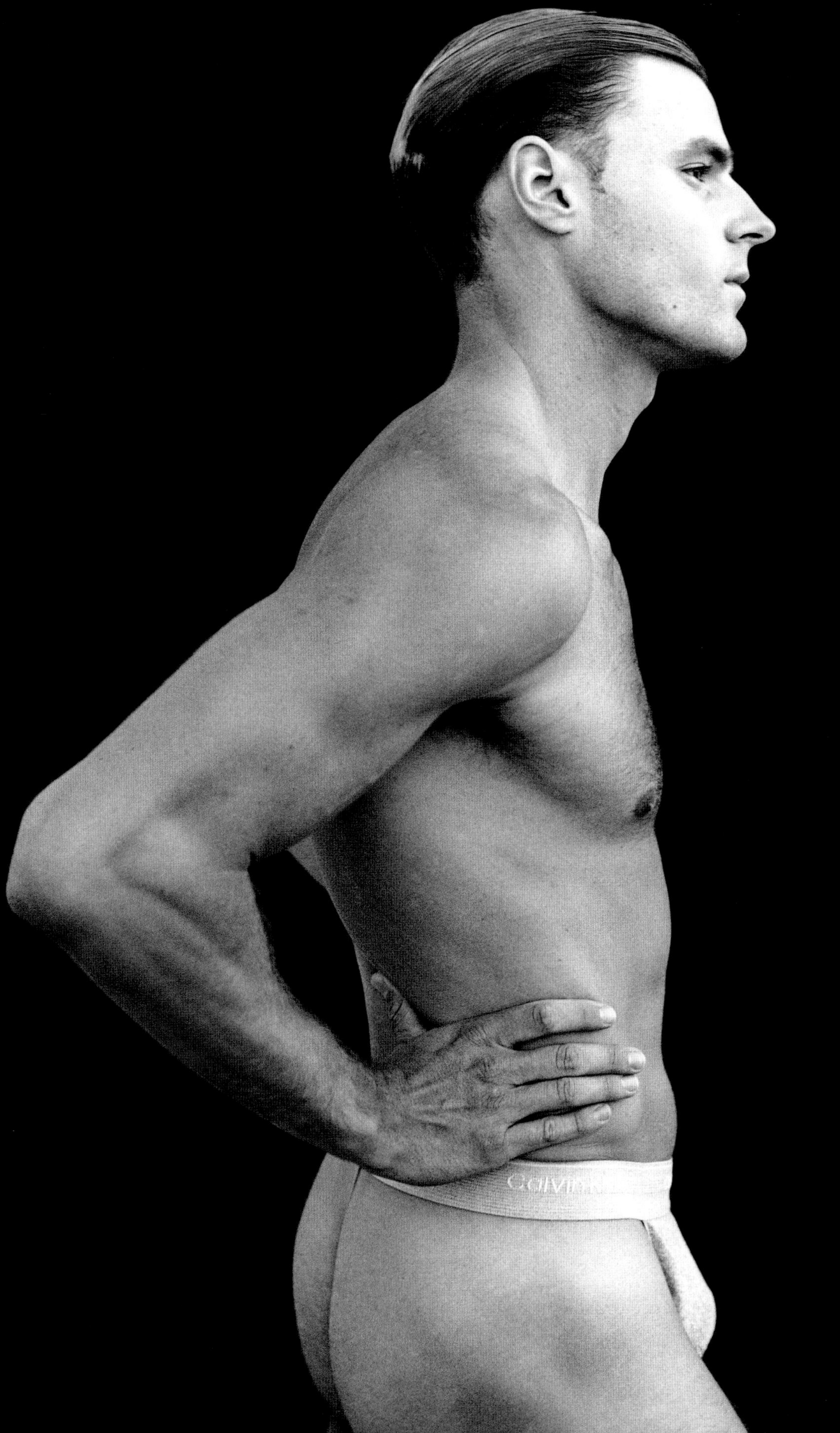

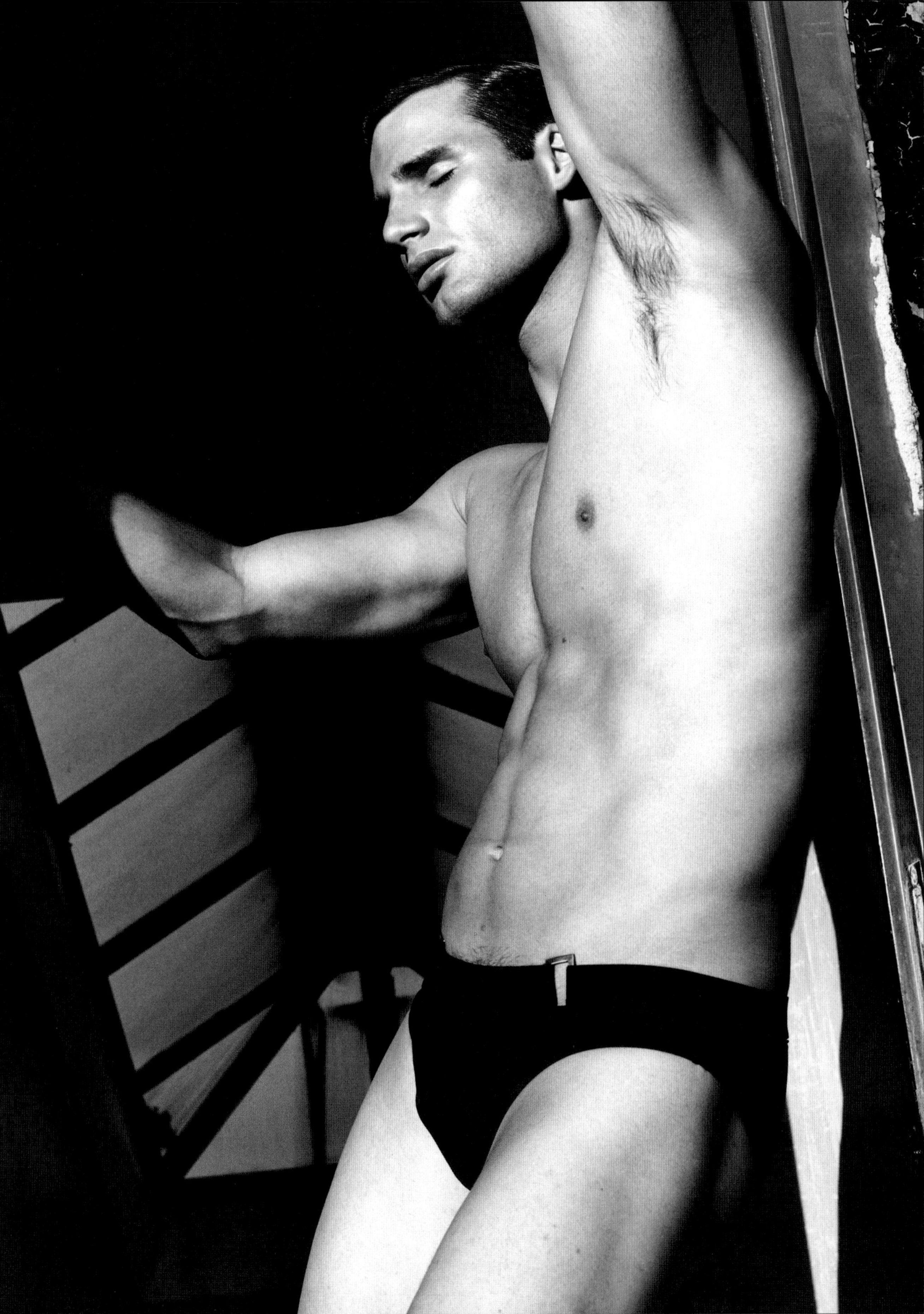

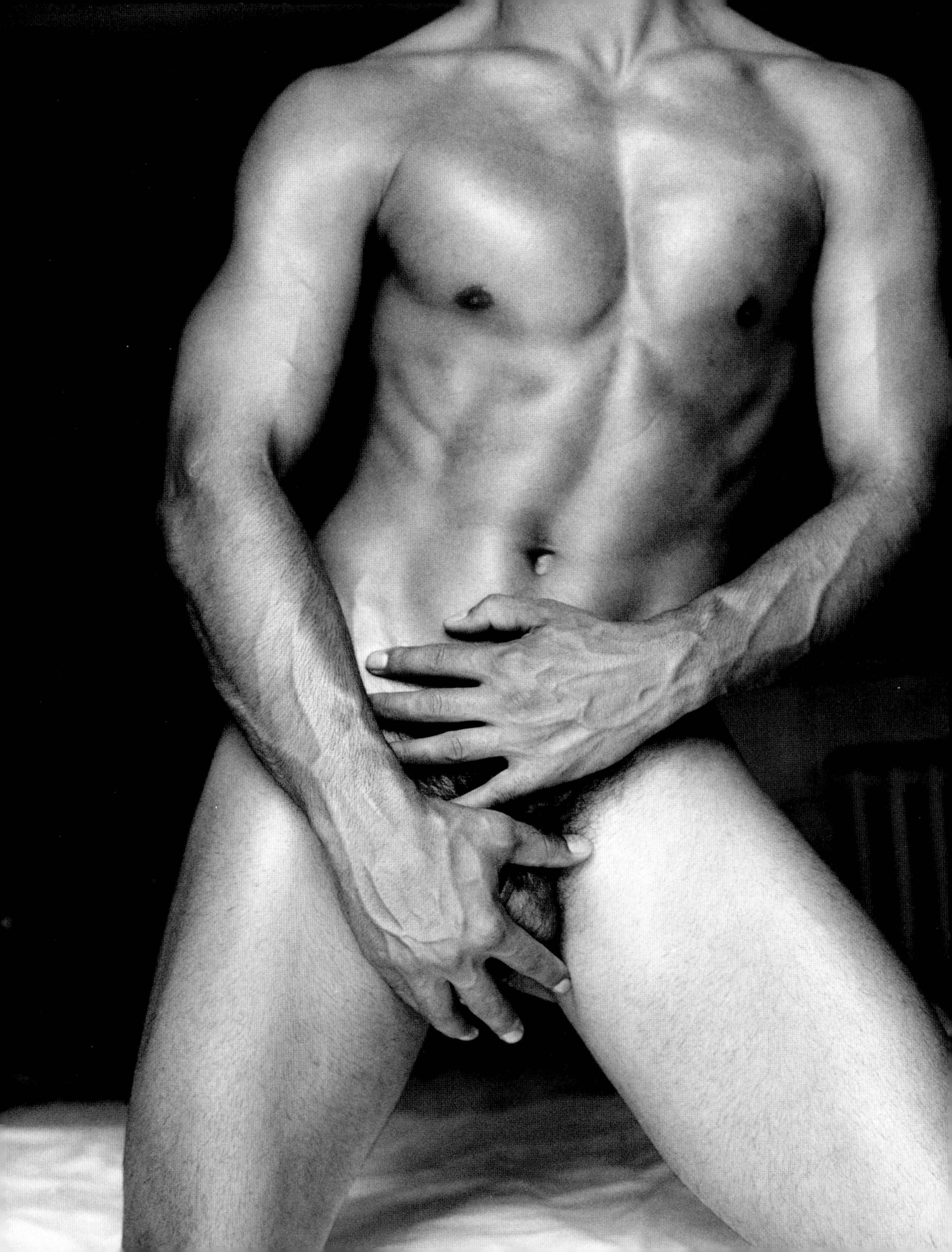

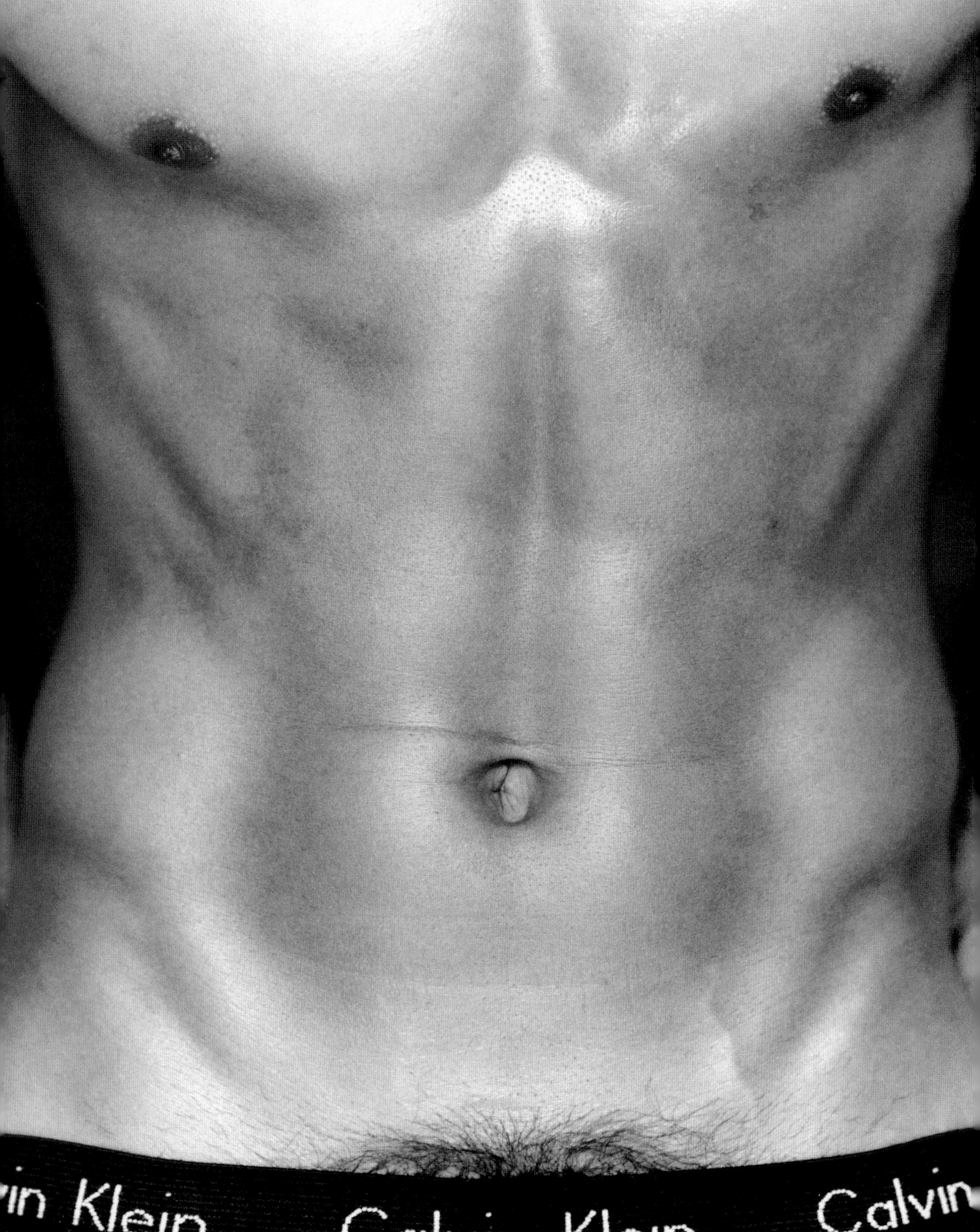
Calvin Klein

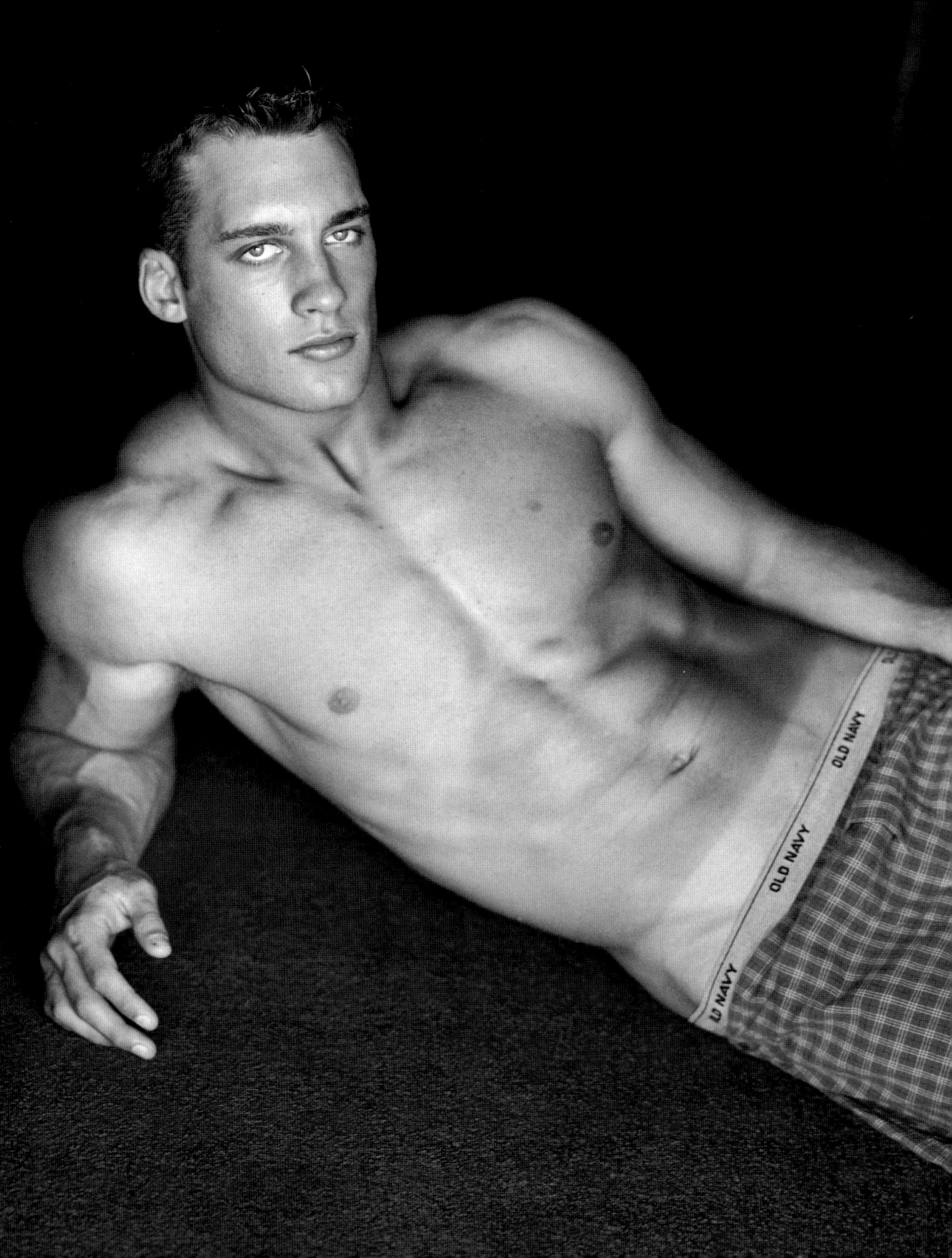

OLD NAVY
OLD NAVY
OLD NAVY
OLD NAVY

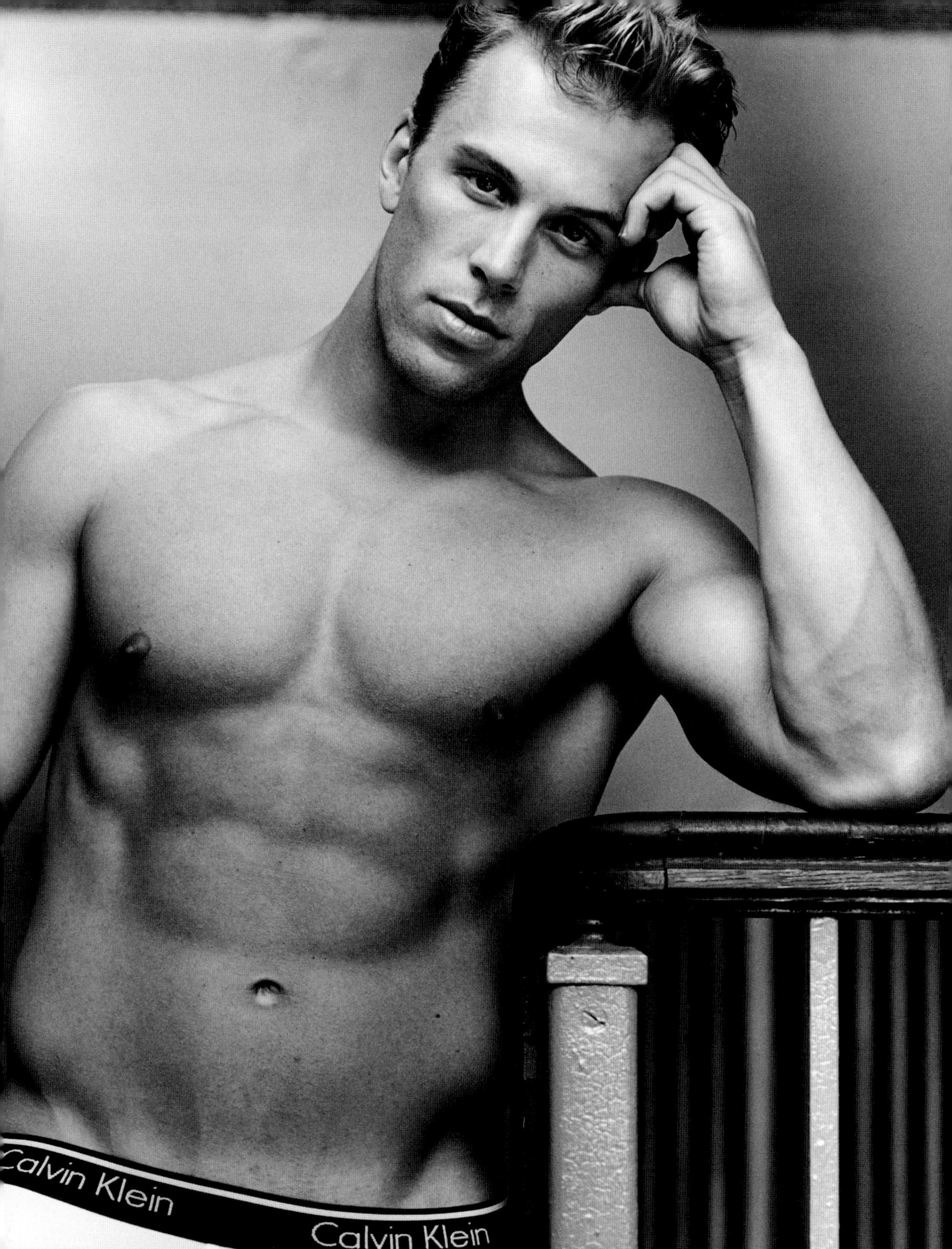
Calvin Klein
Calvin Klein

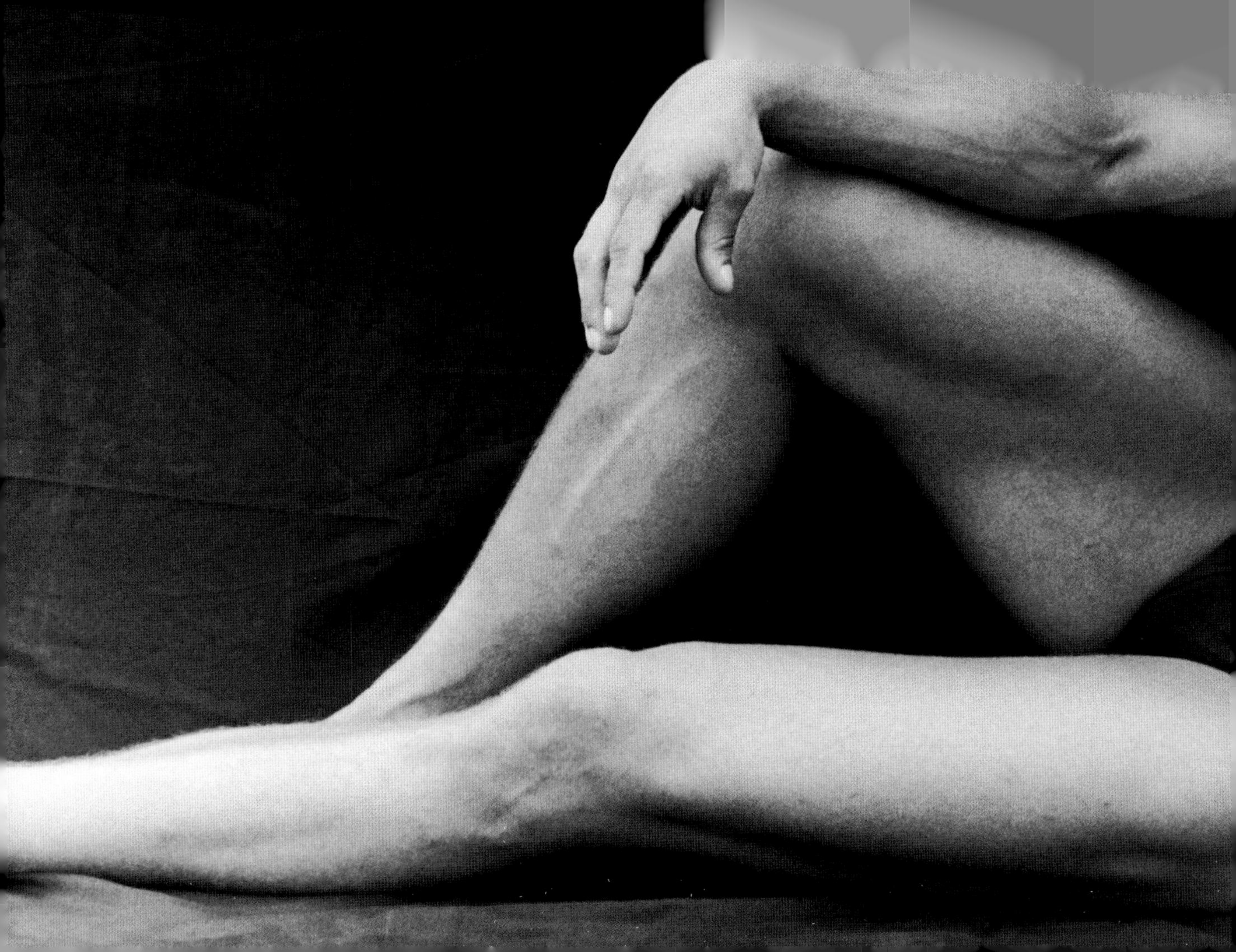

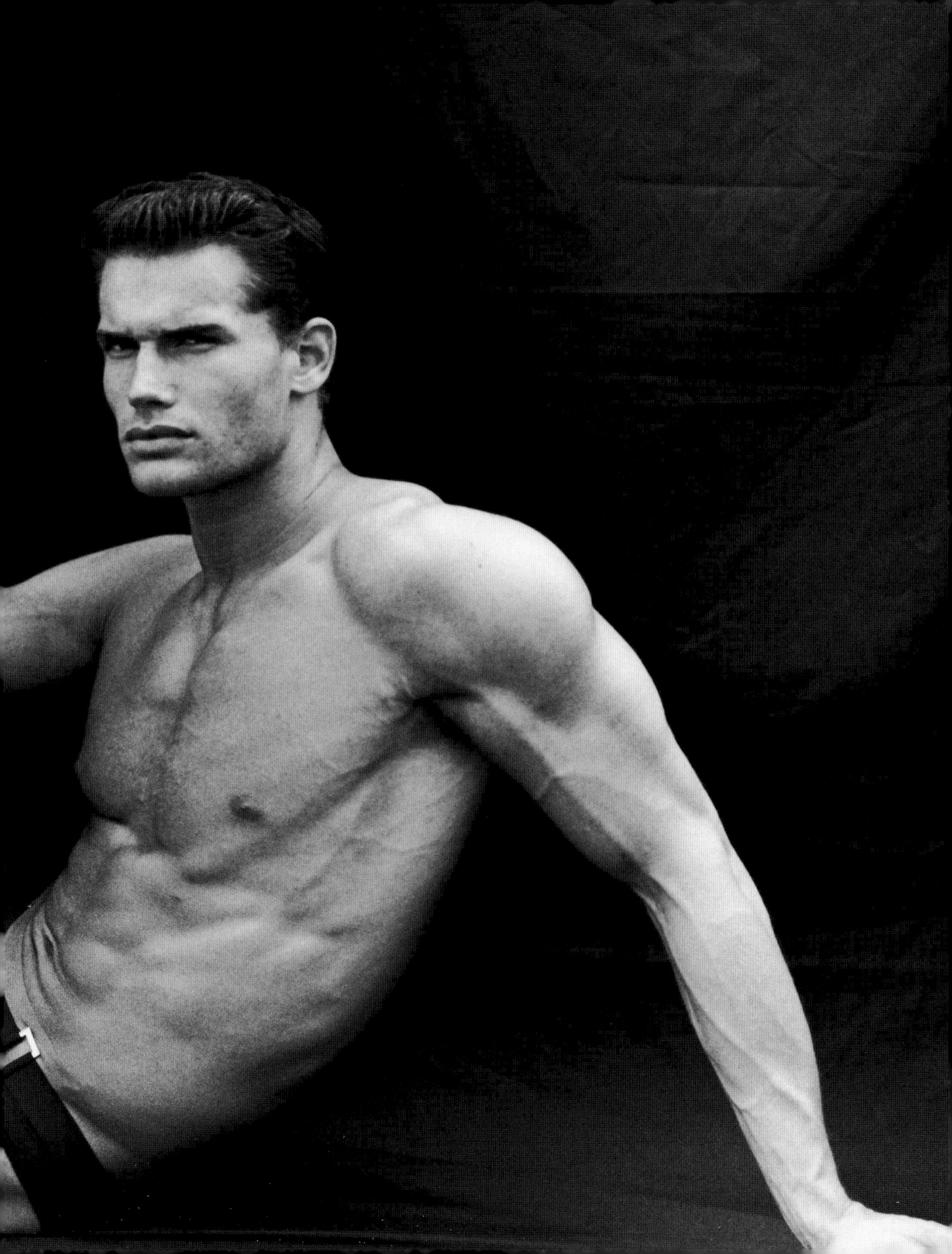

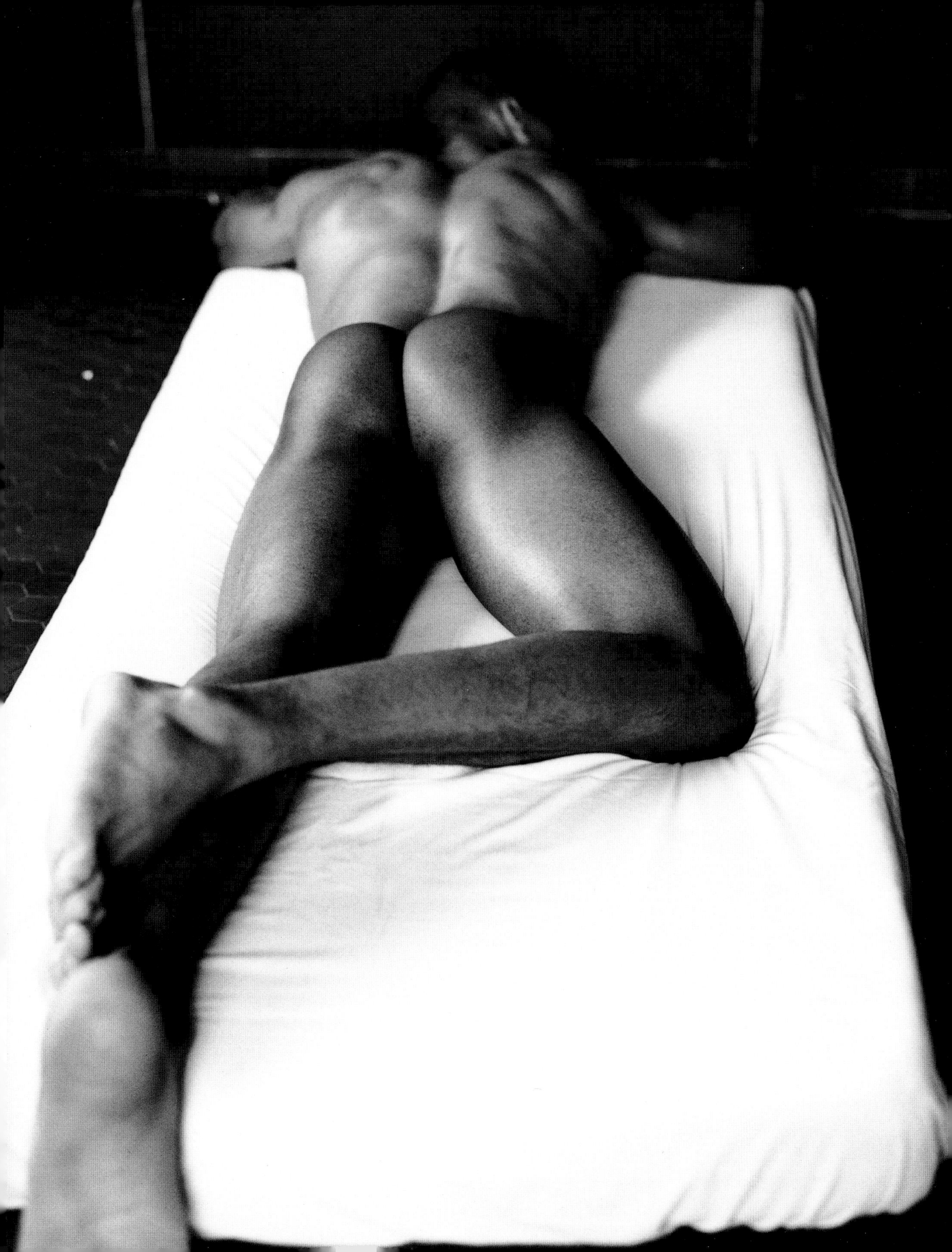

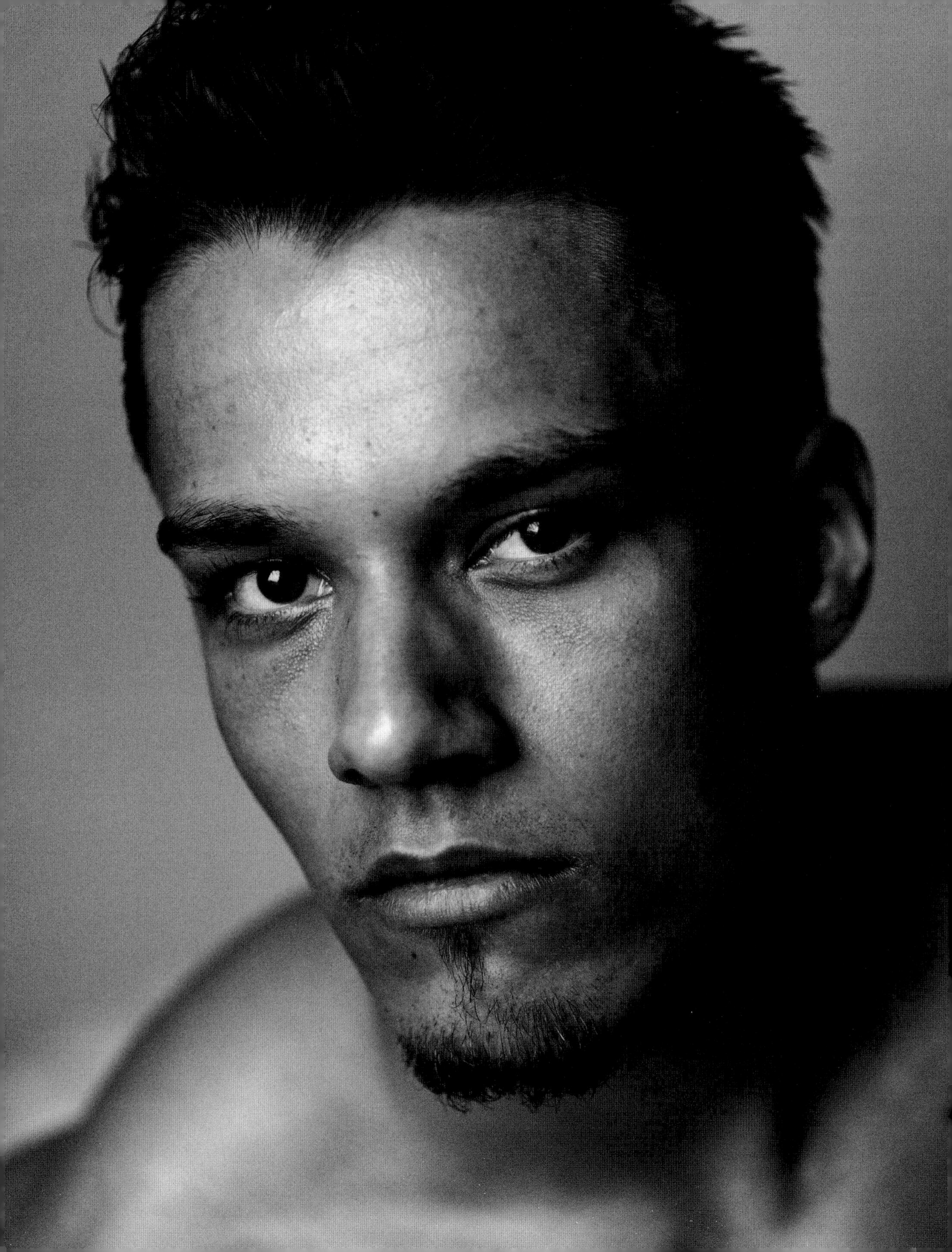

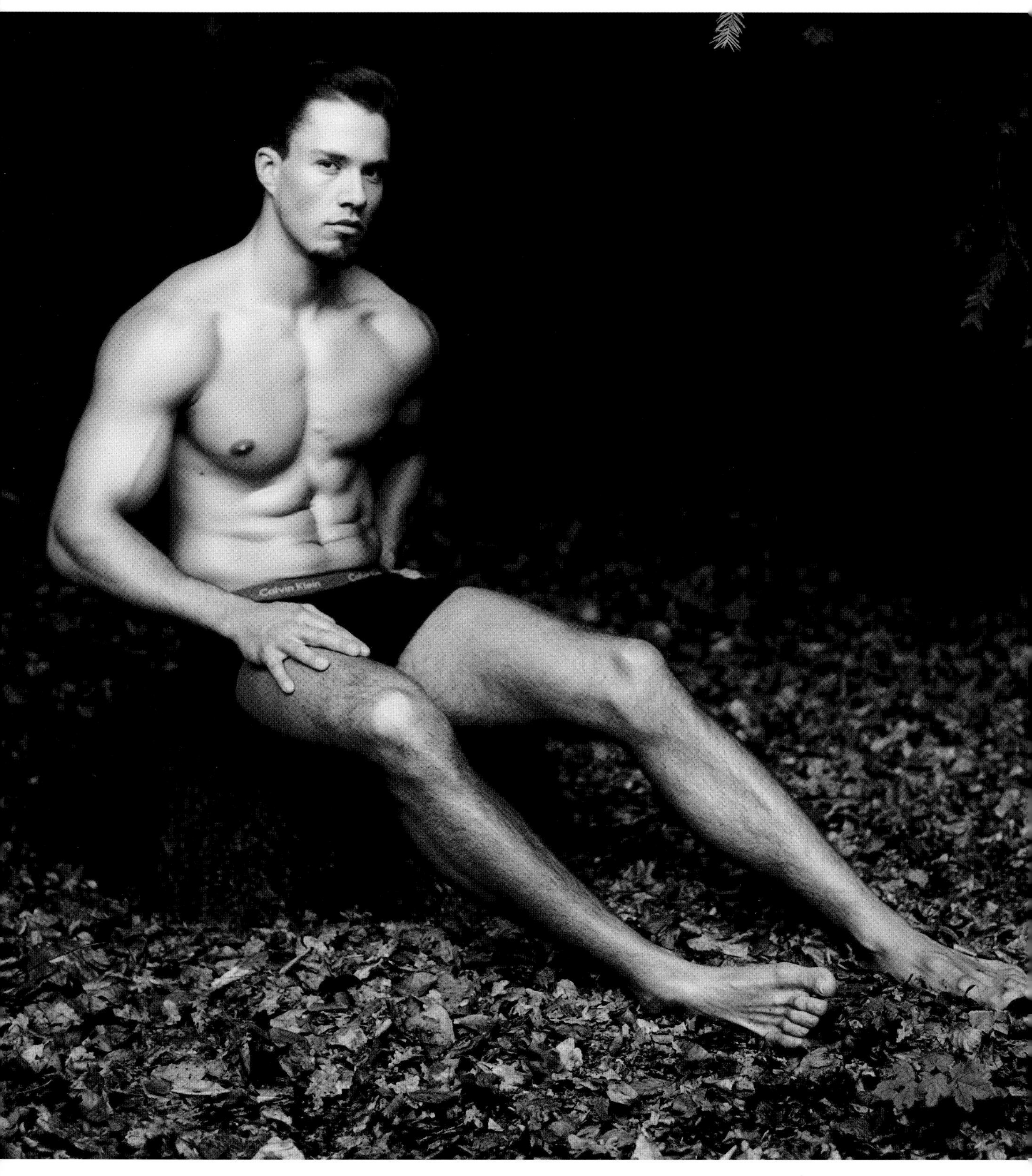

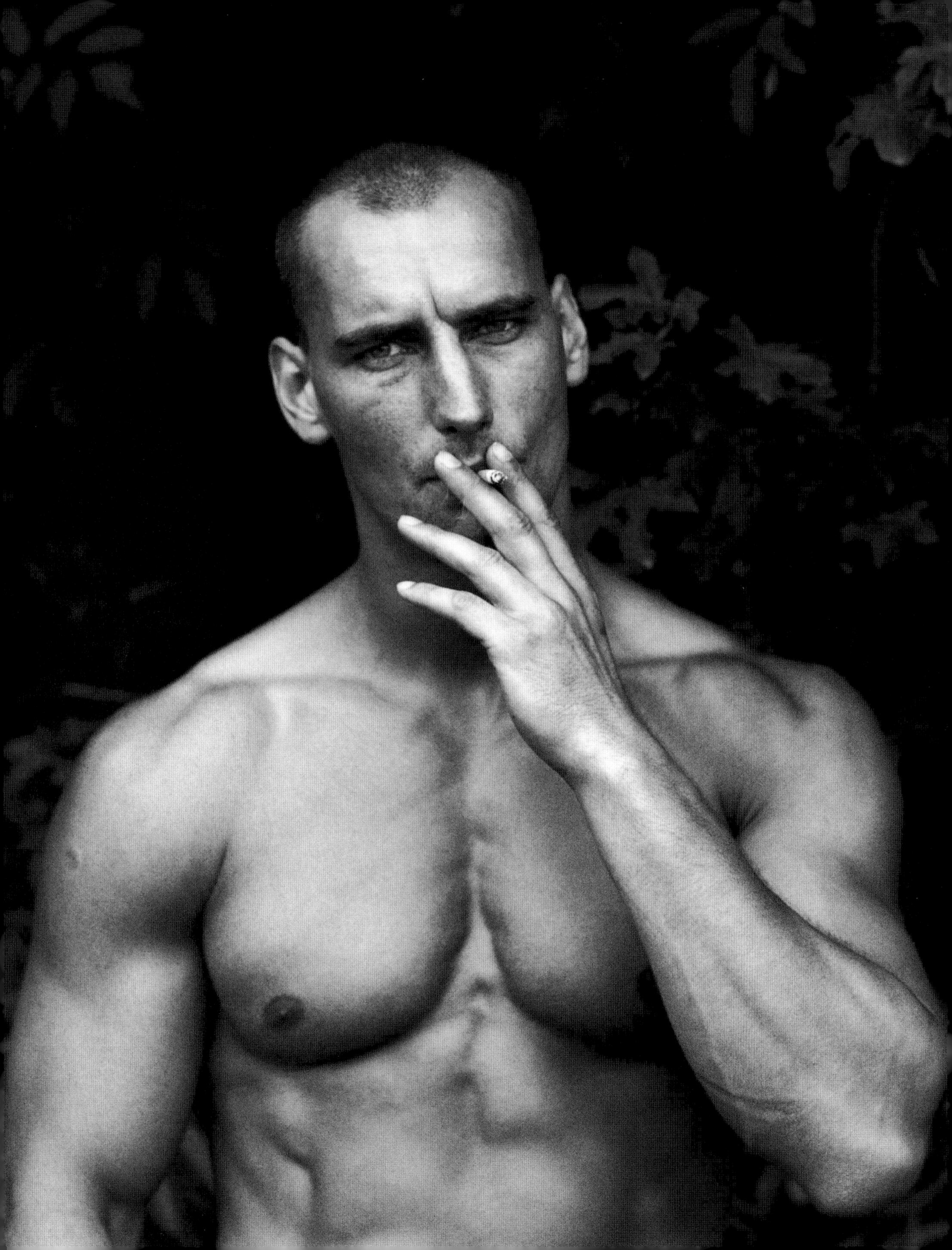

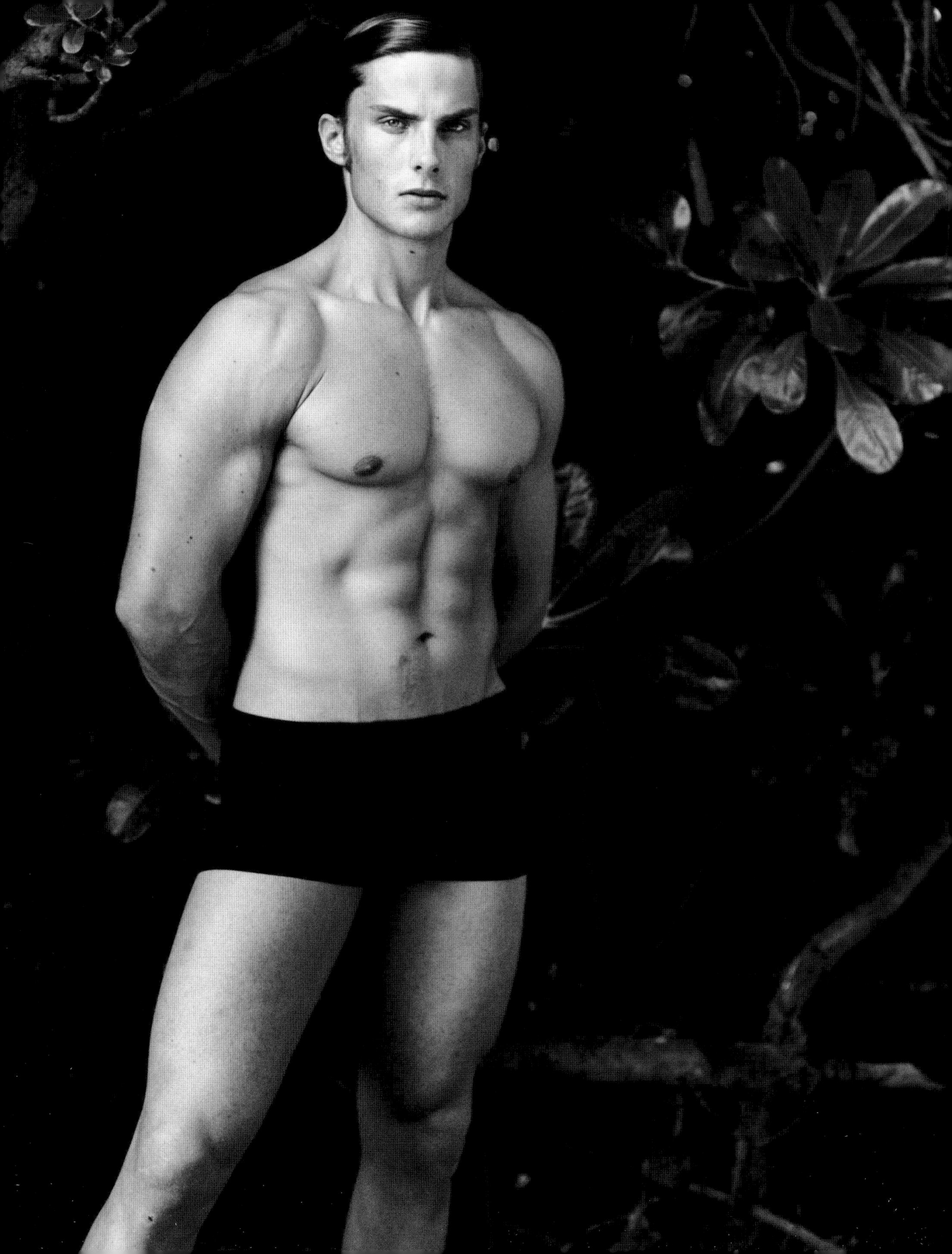

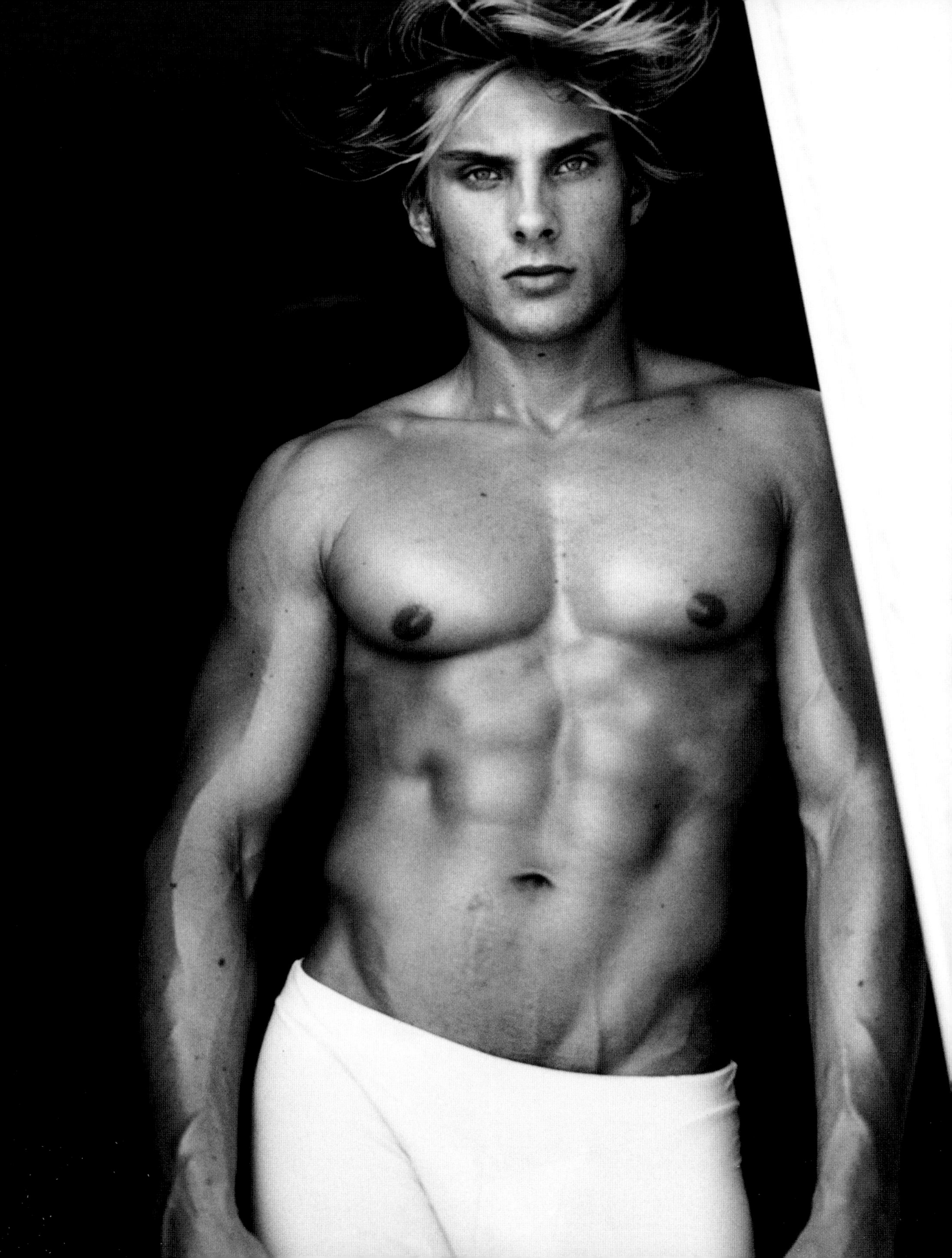

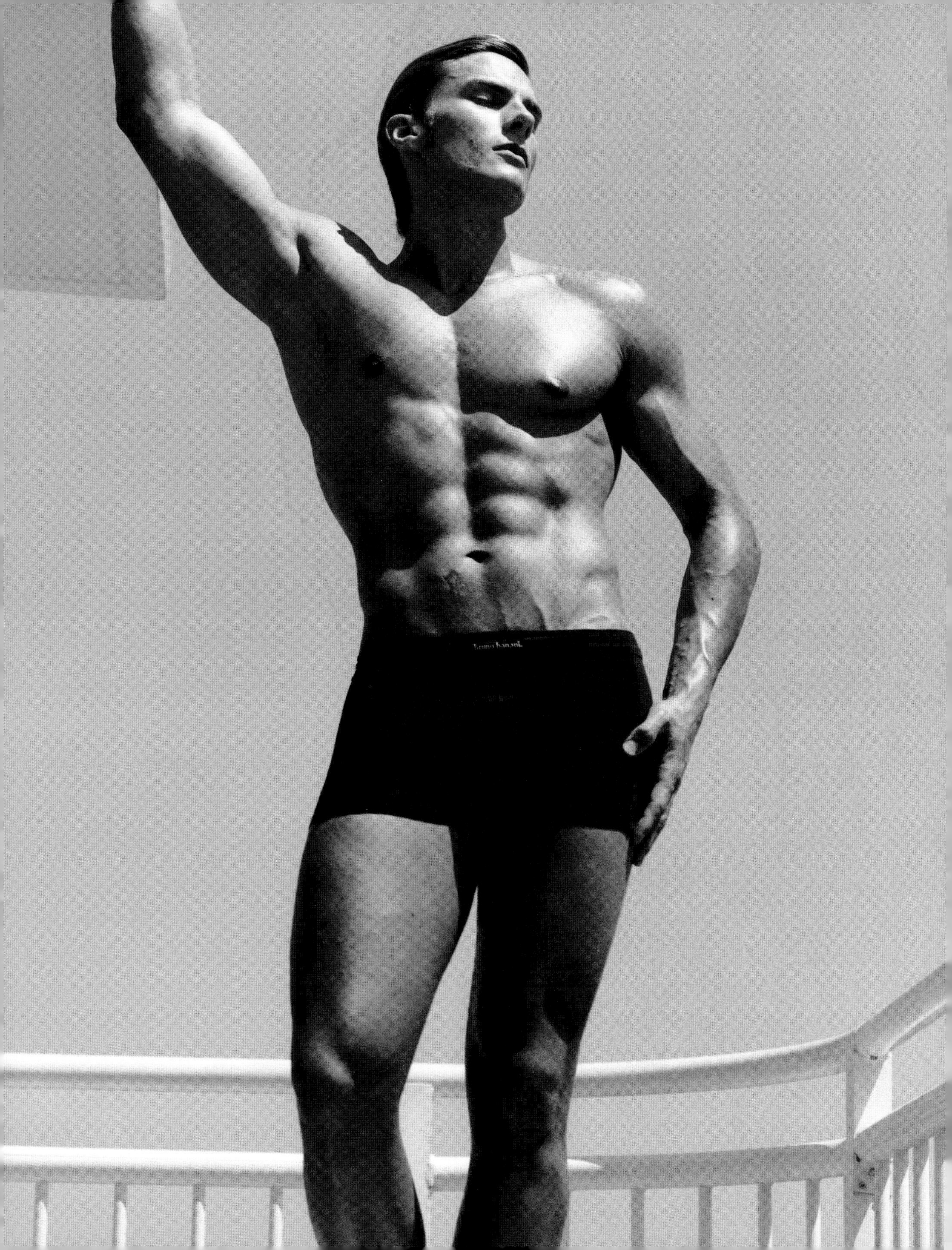

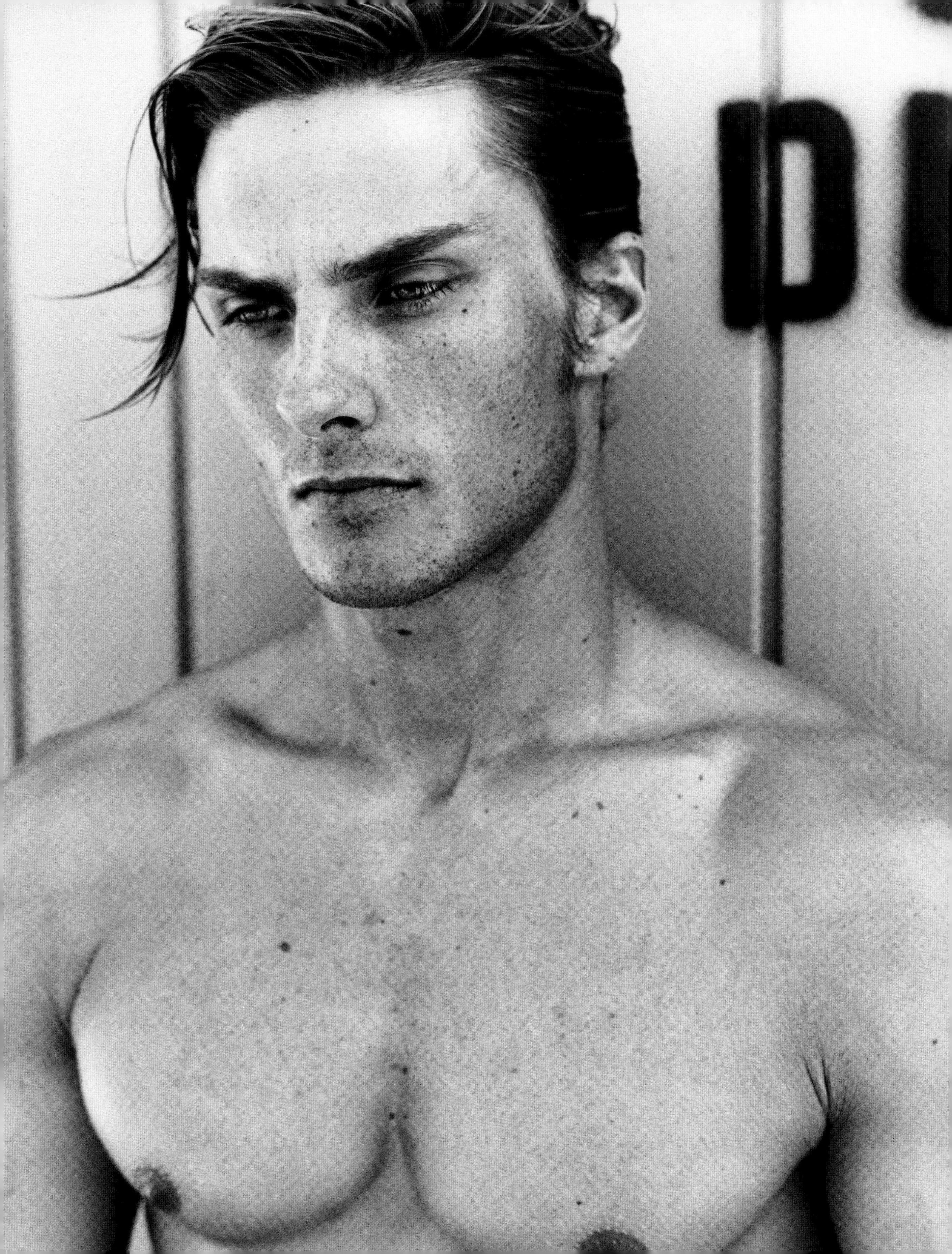

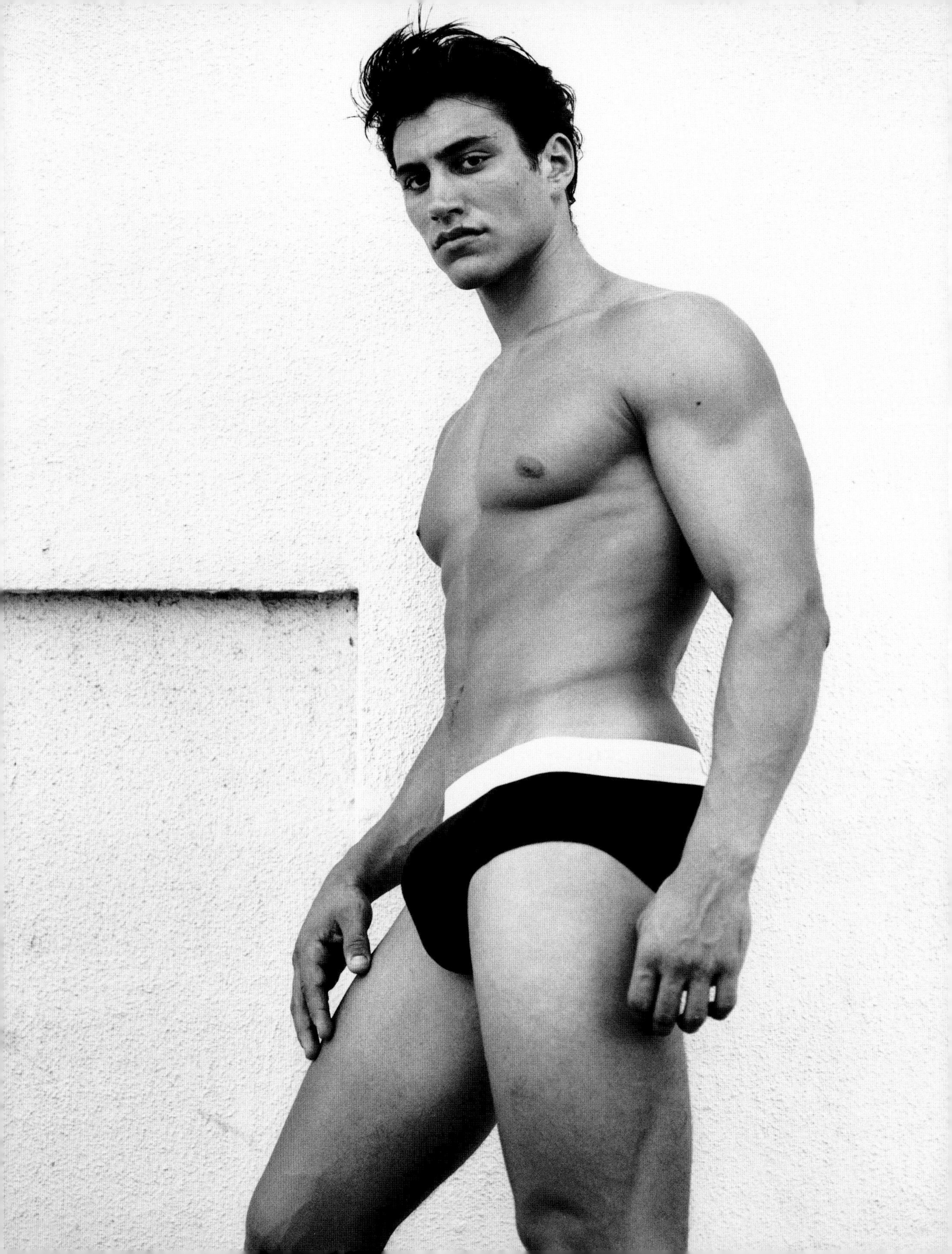

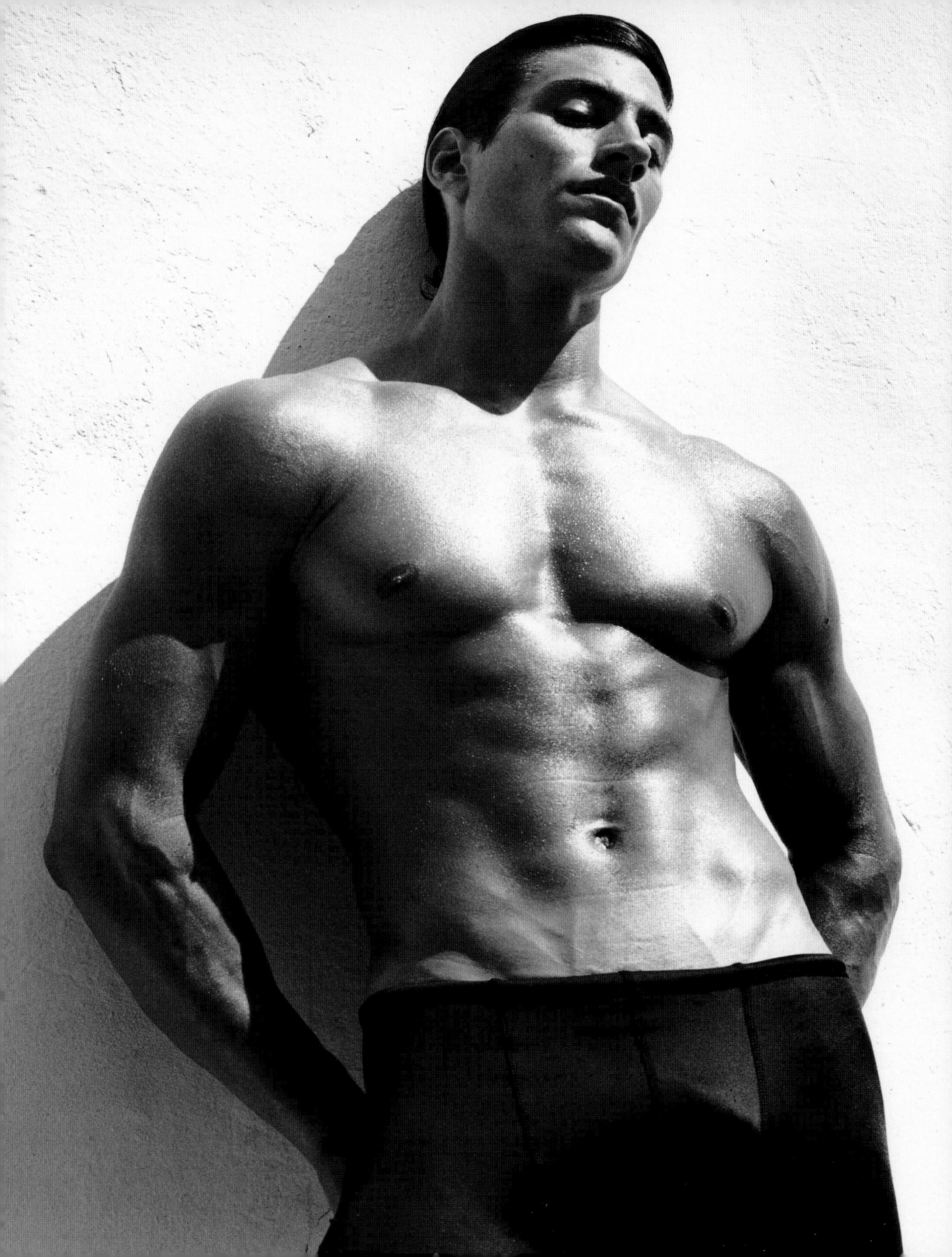

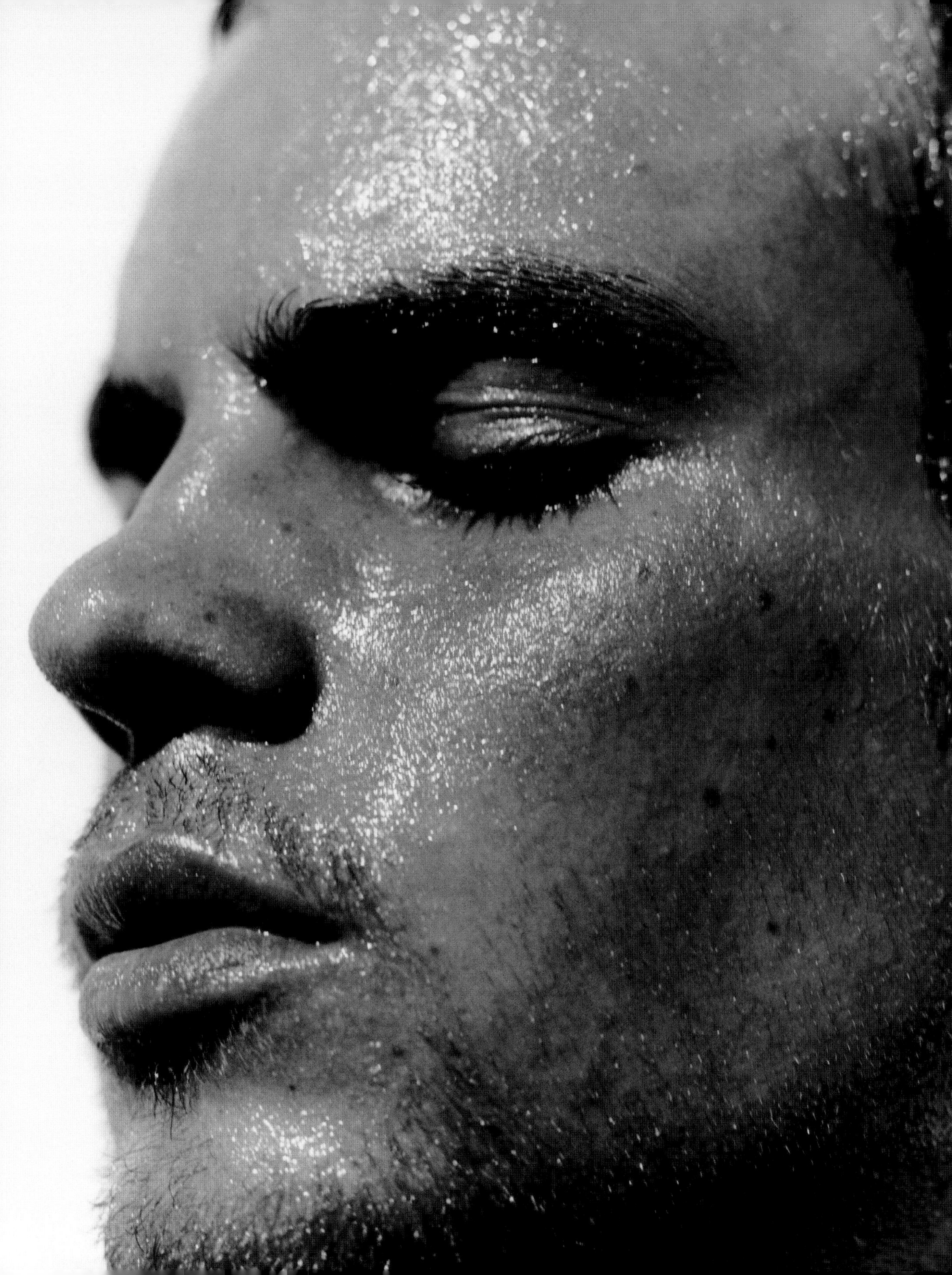

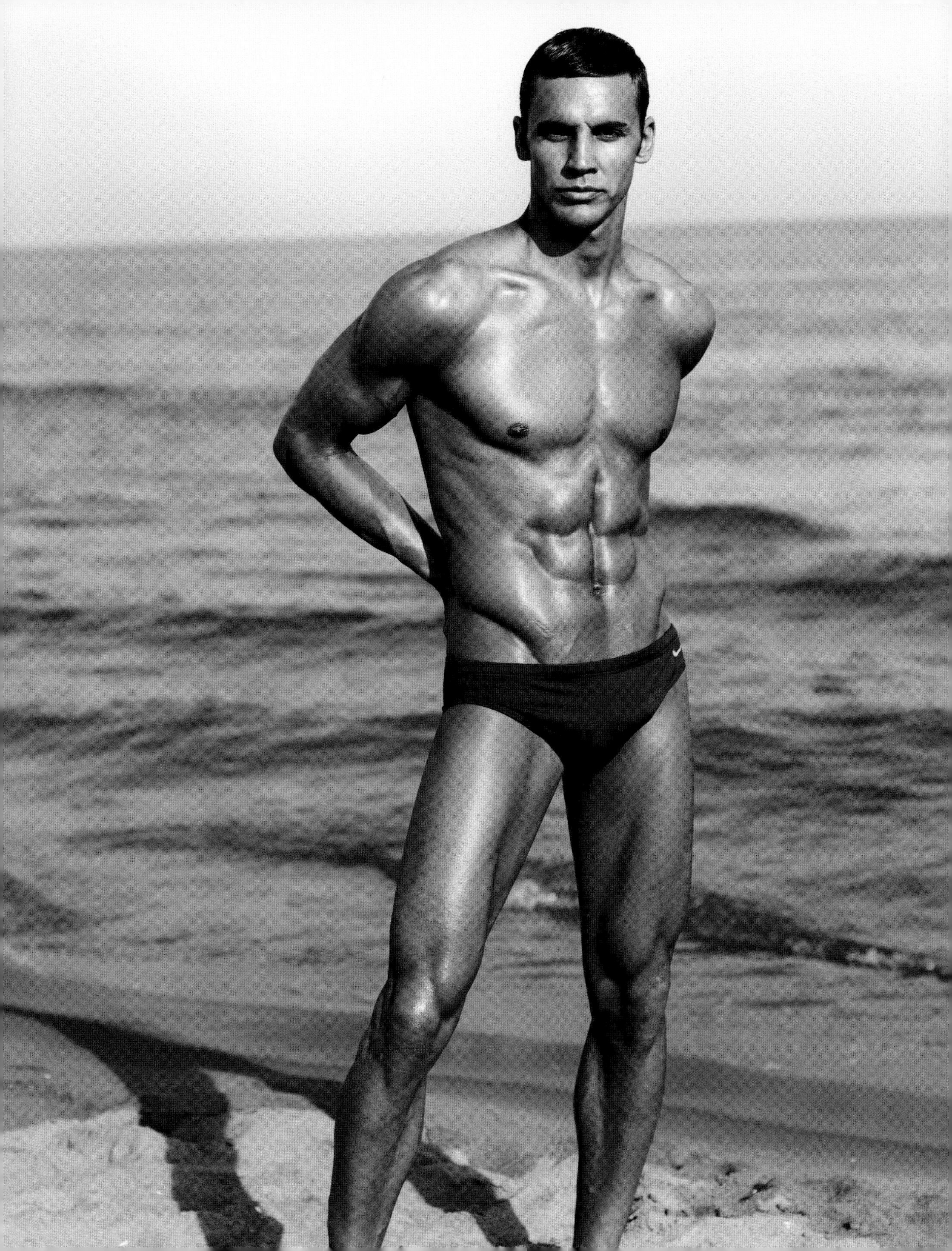

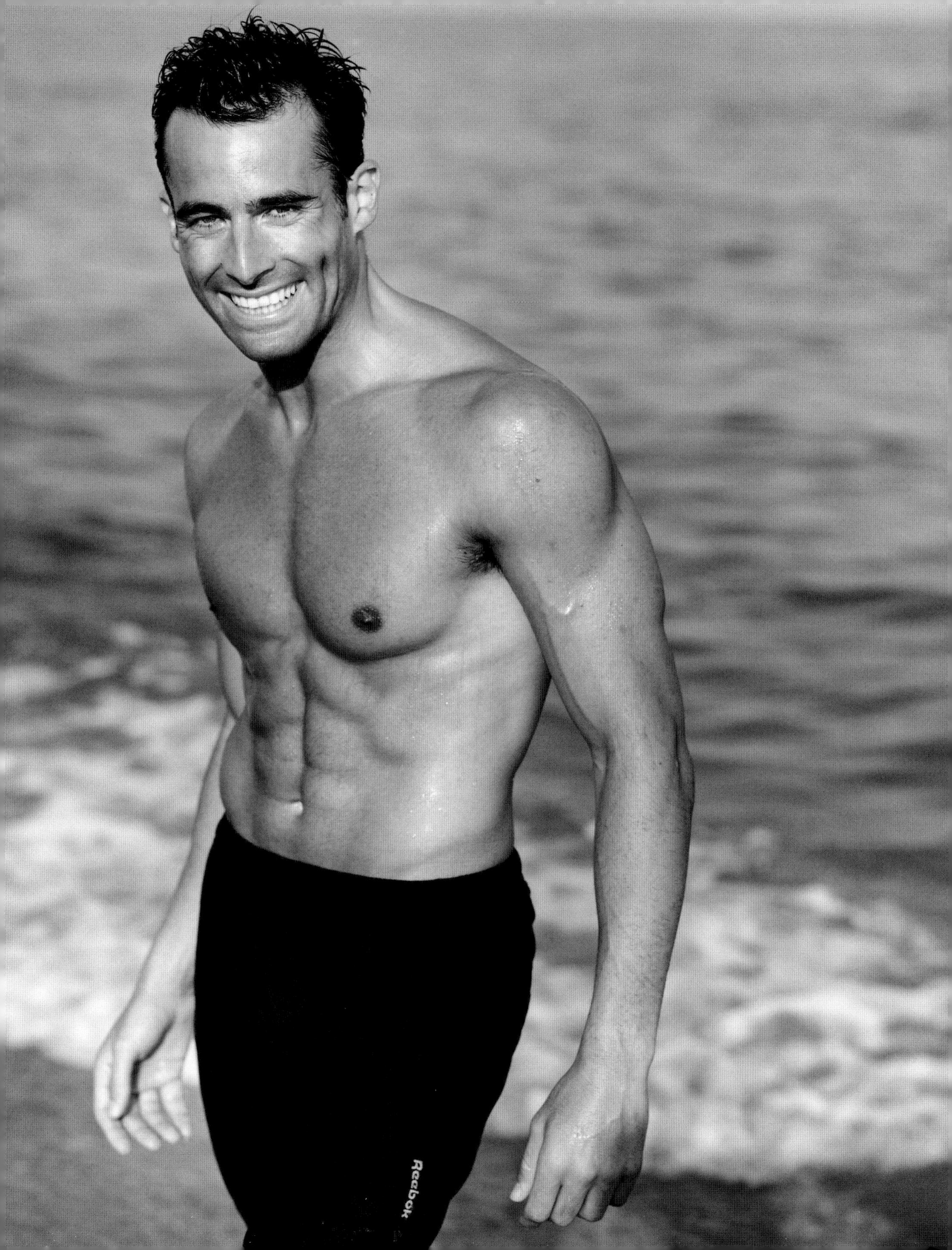

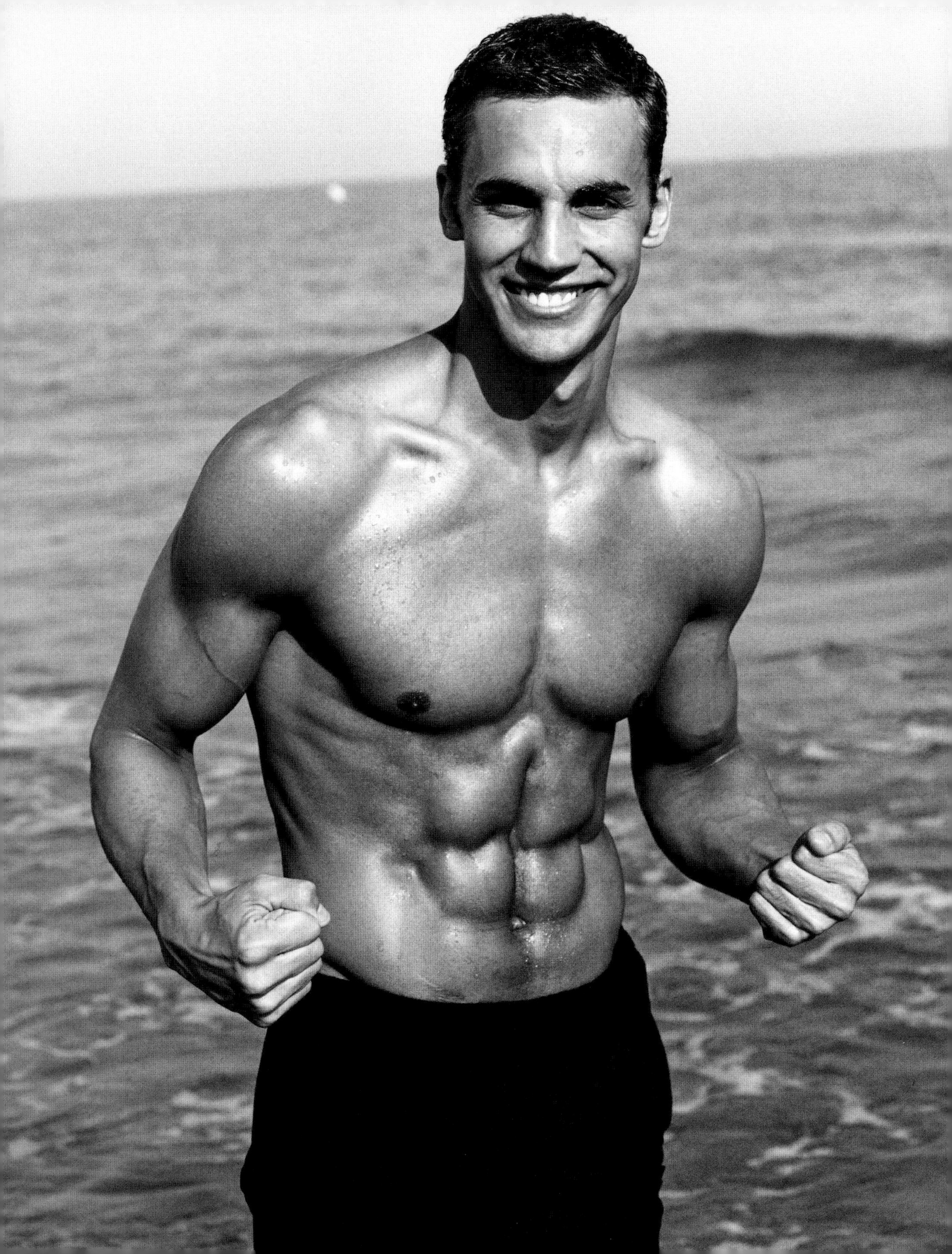

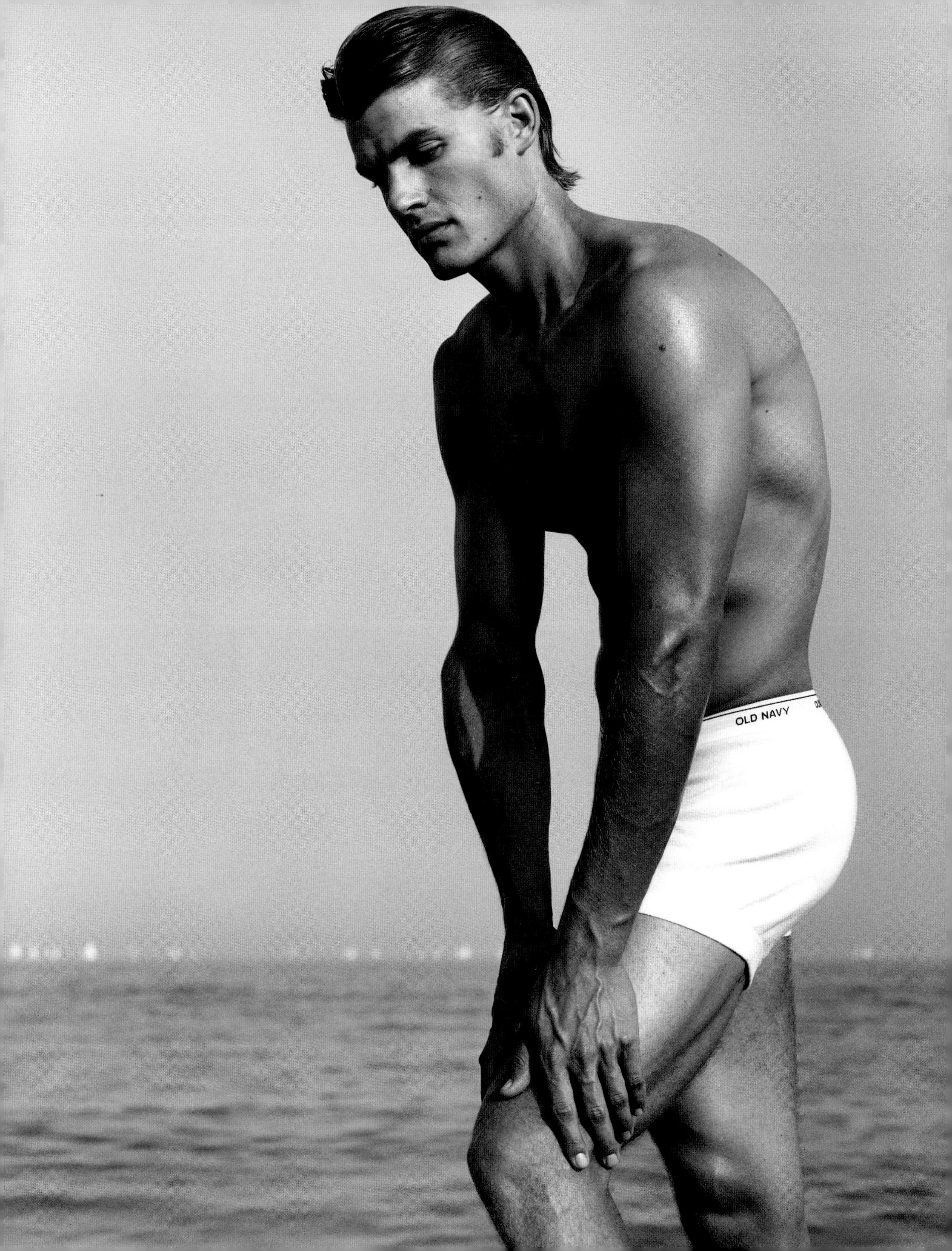

OLD NAVY

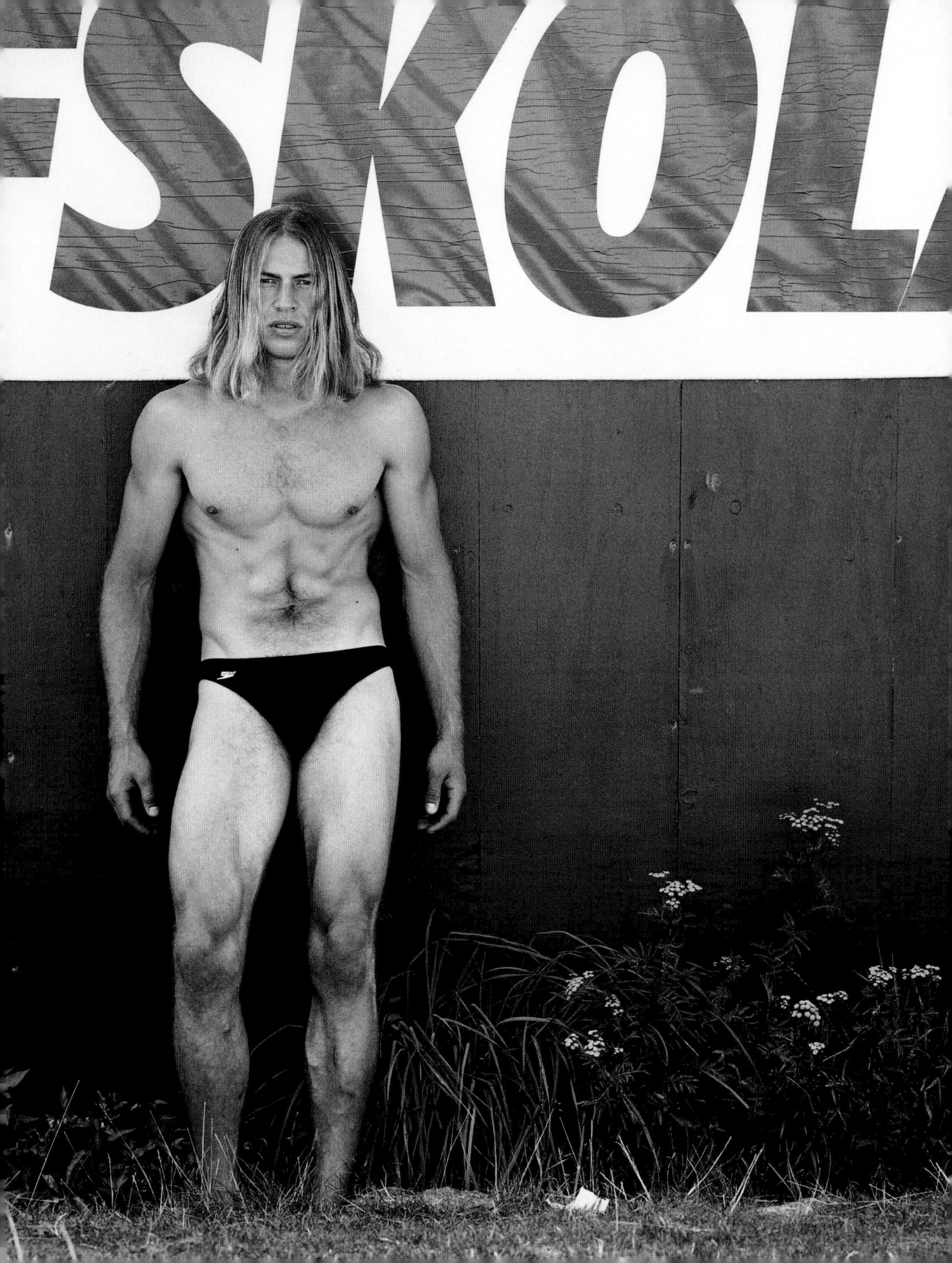
ESSKOL

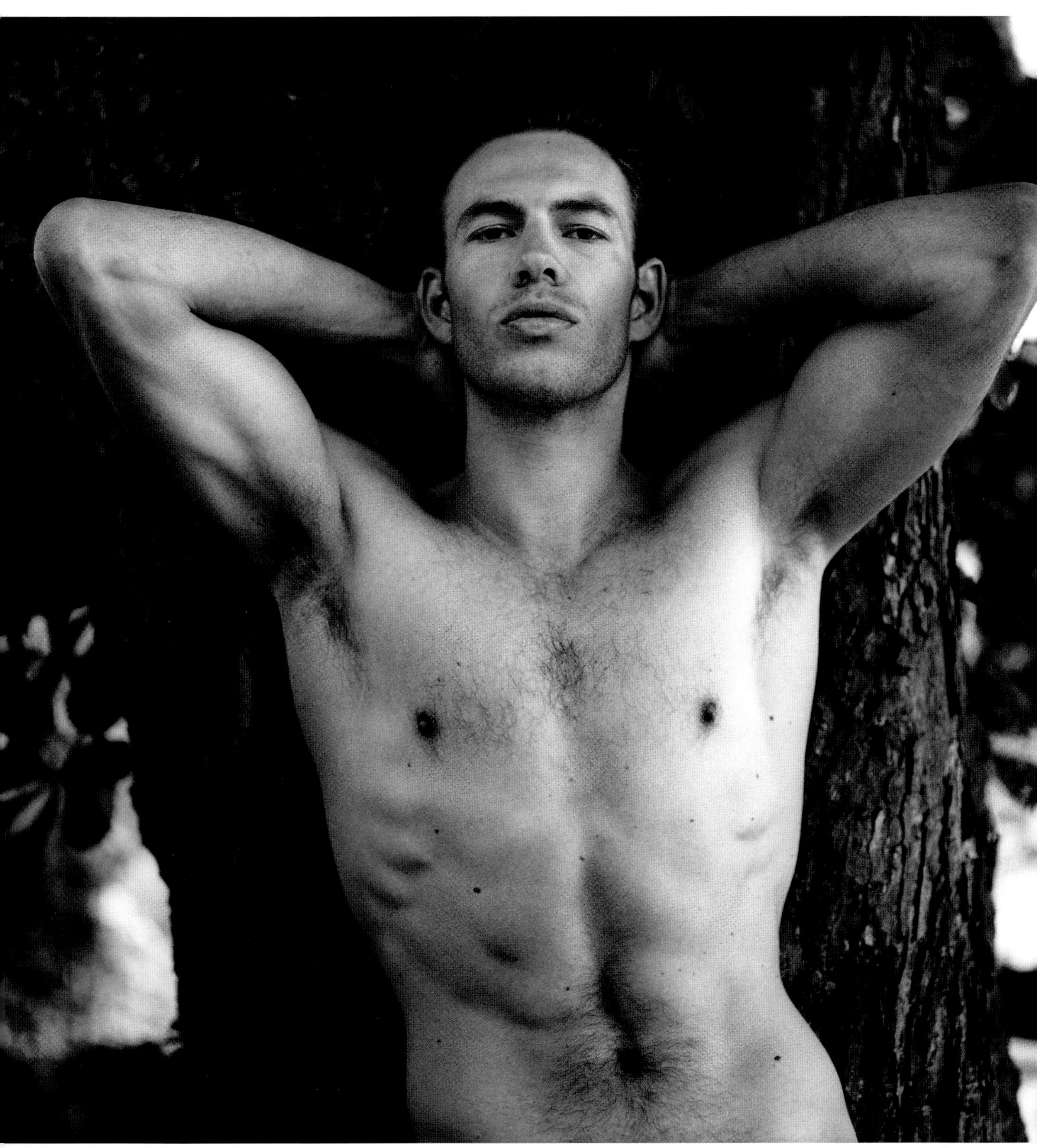

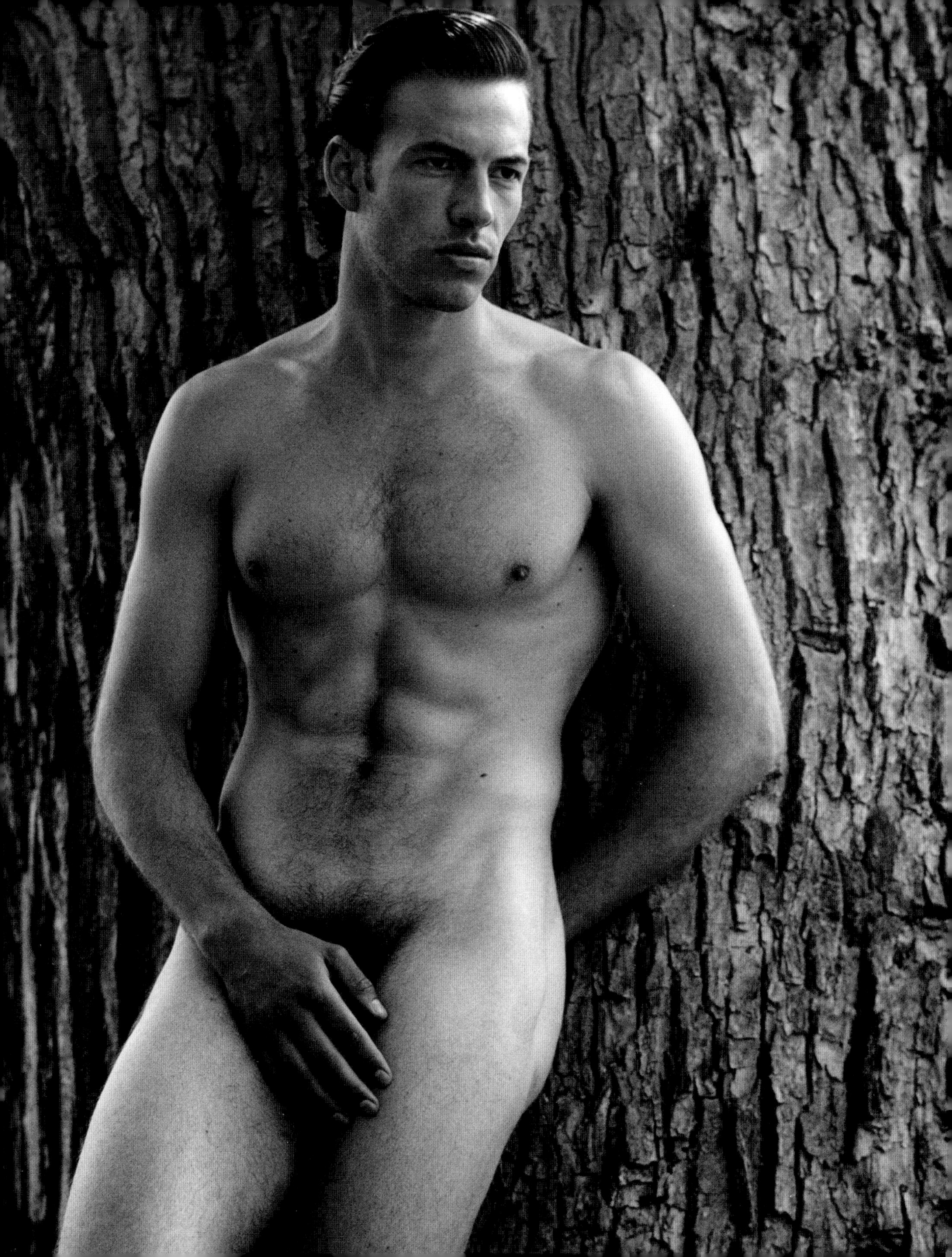

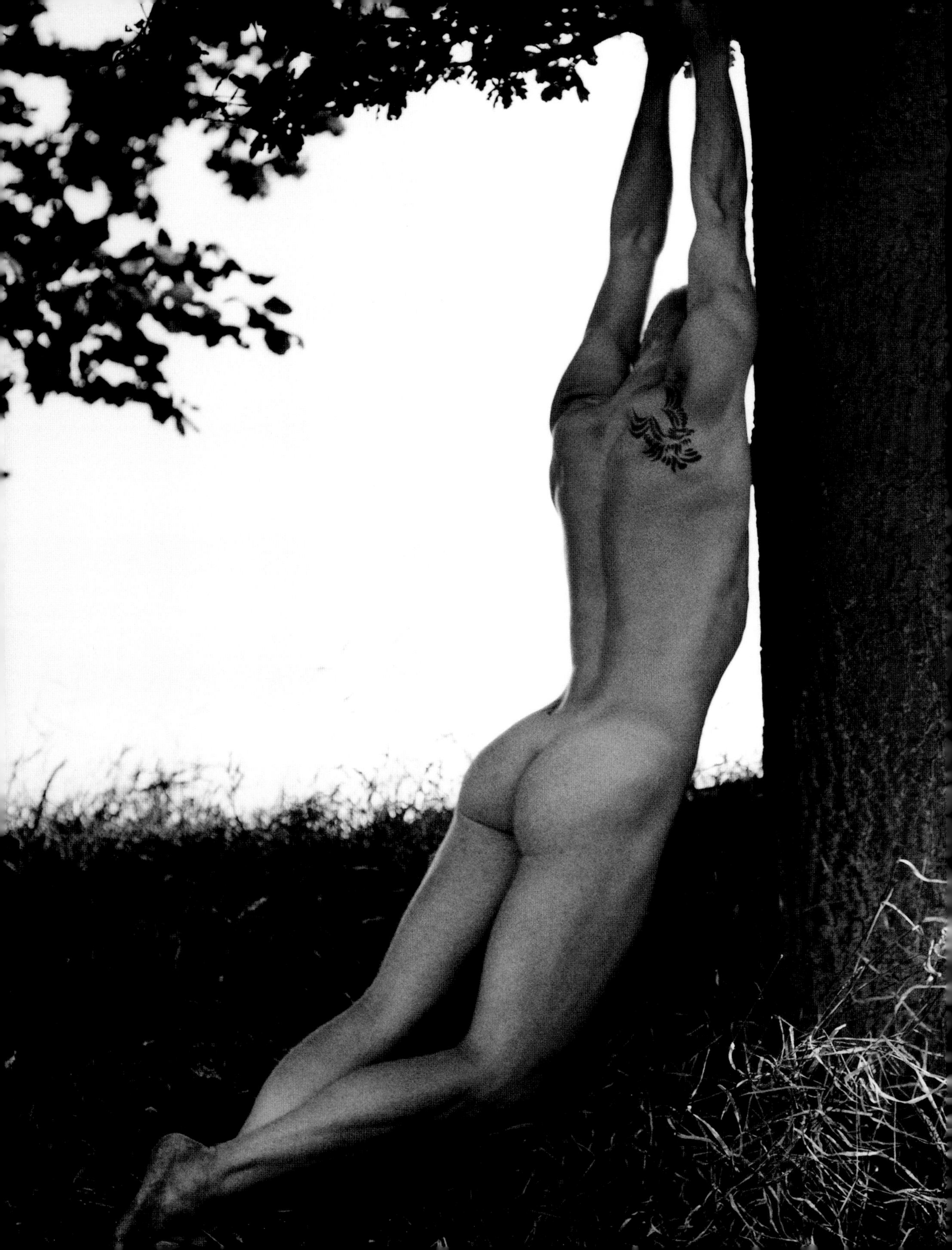

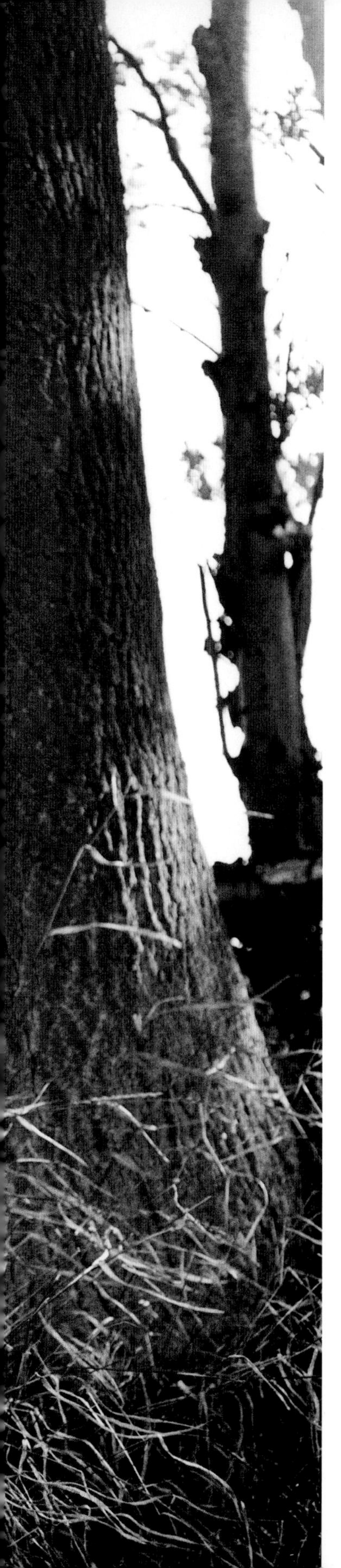

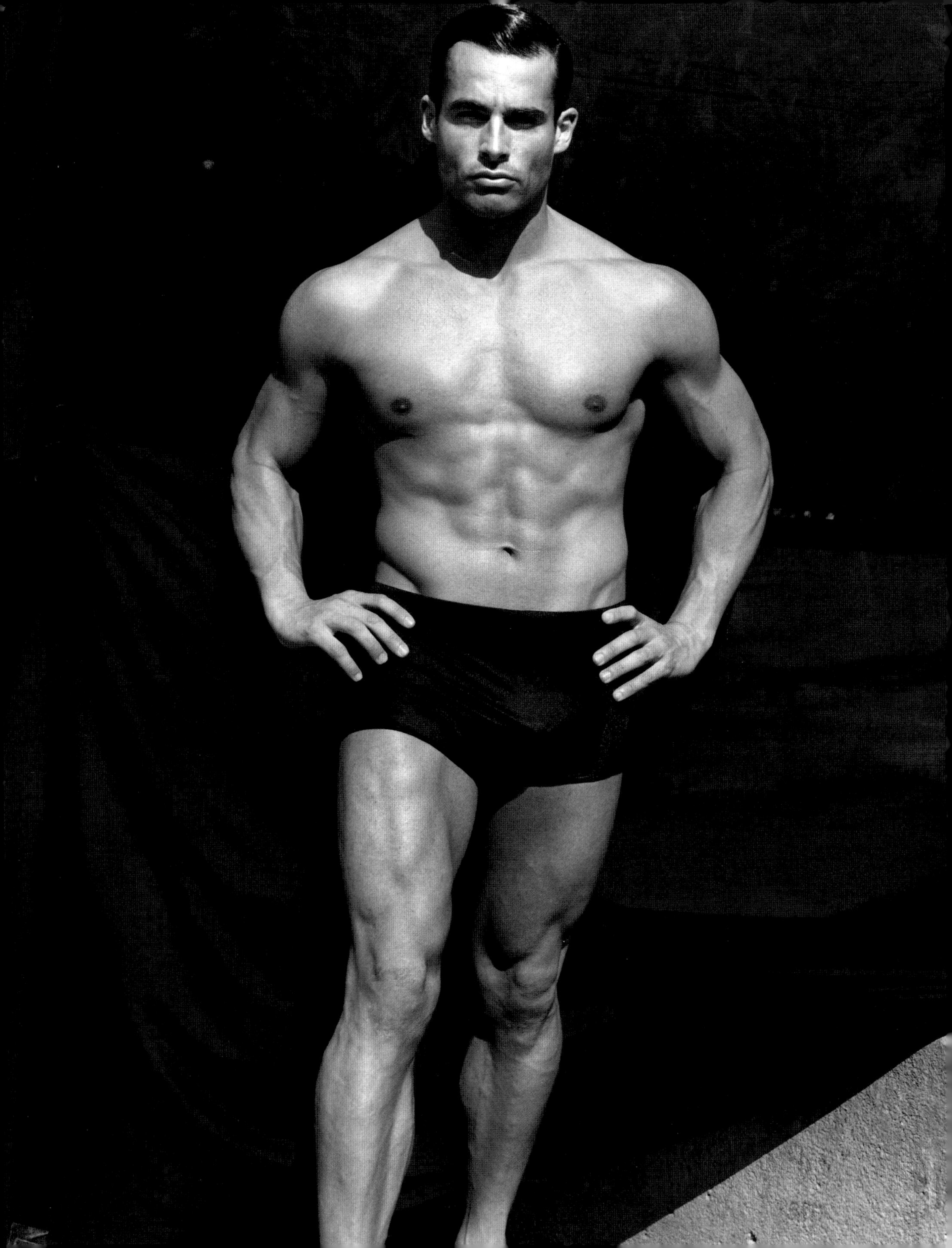

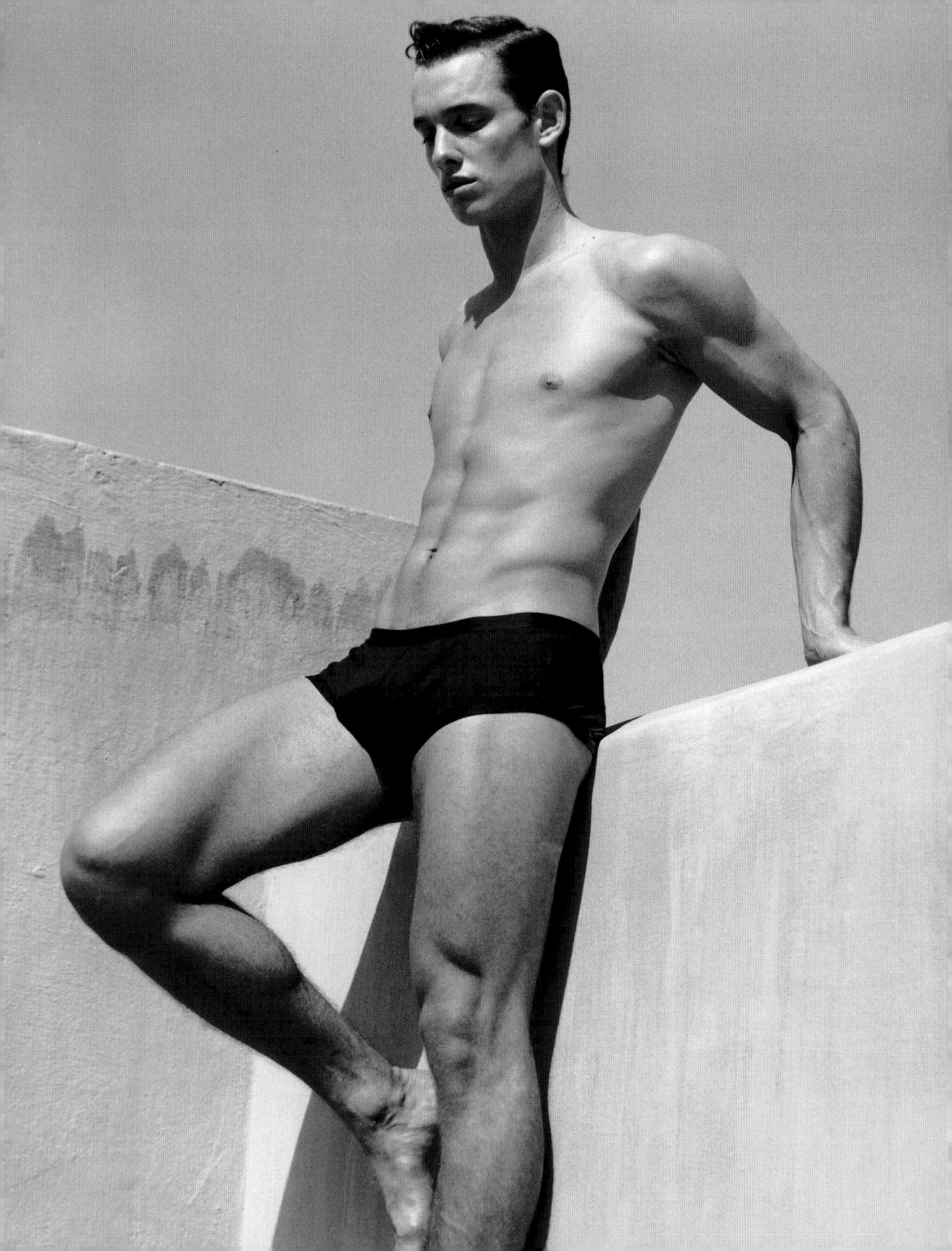

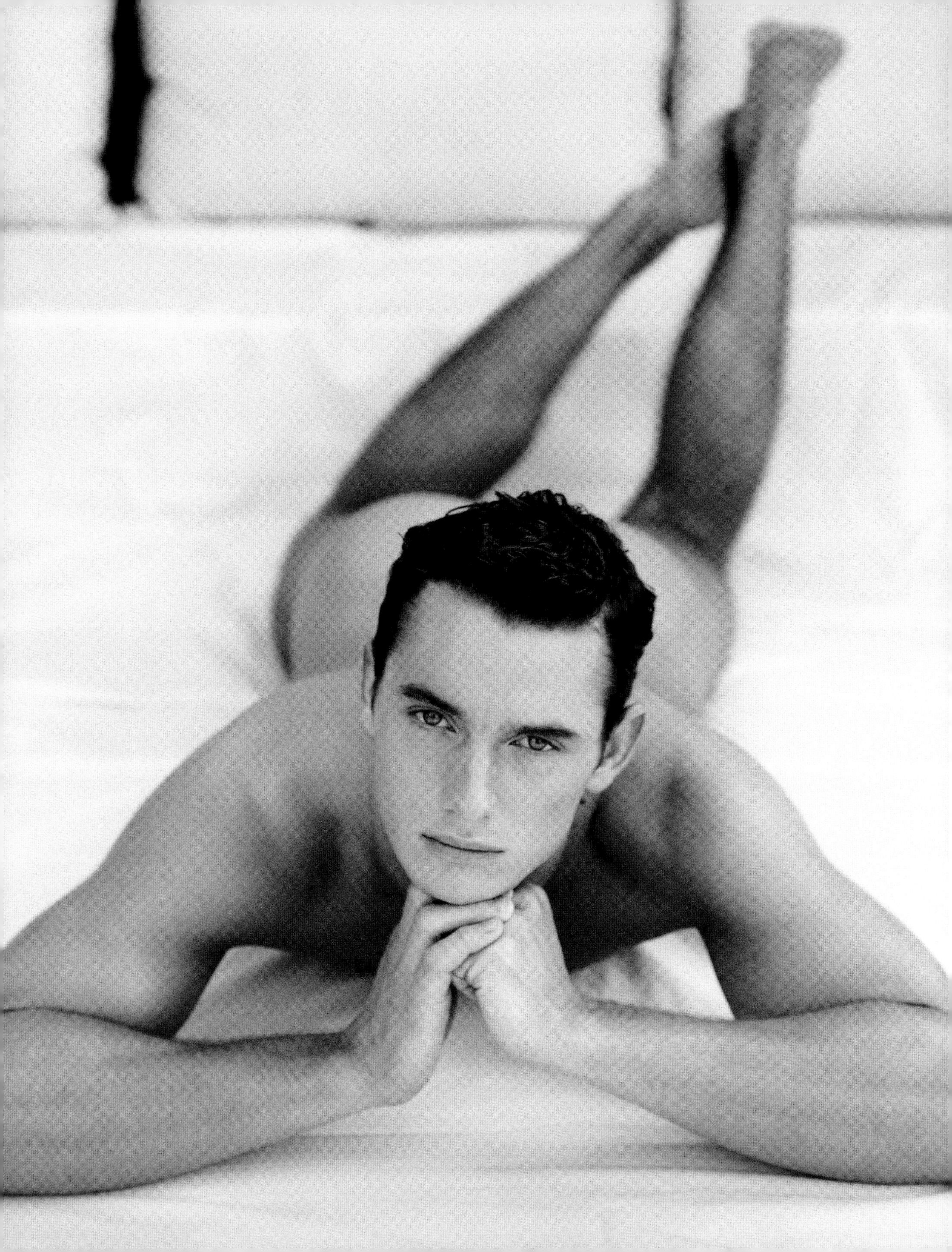

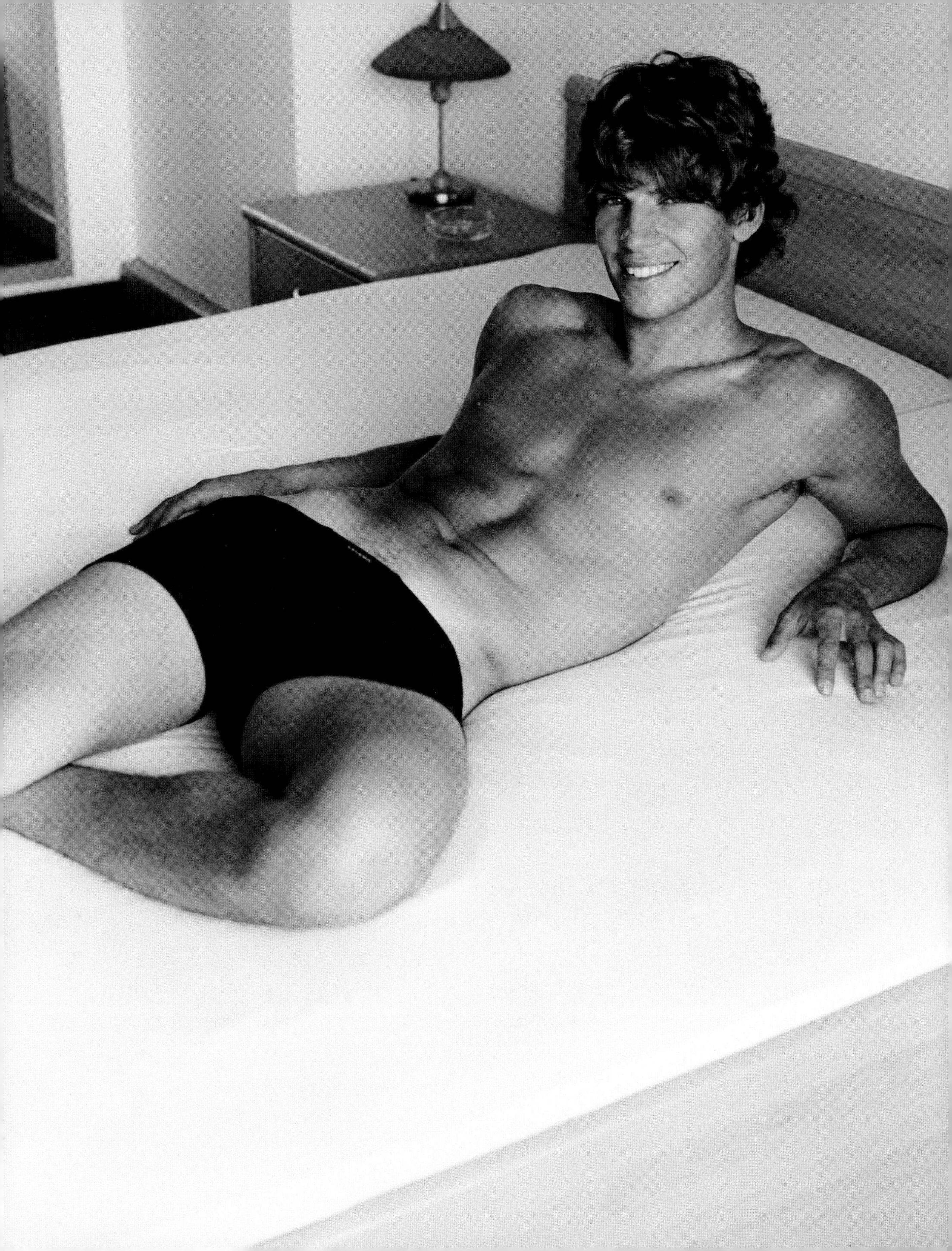

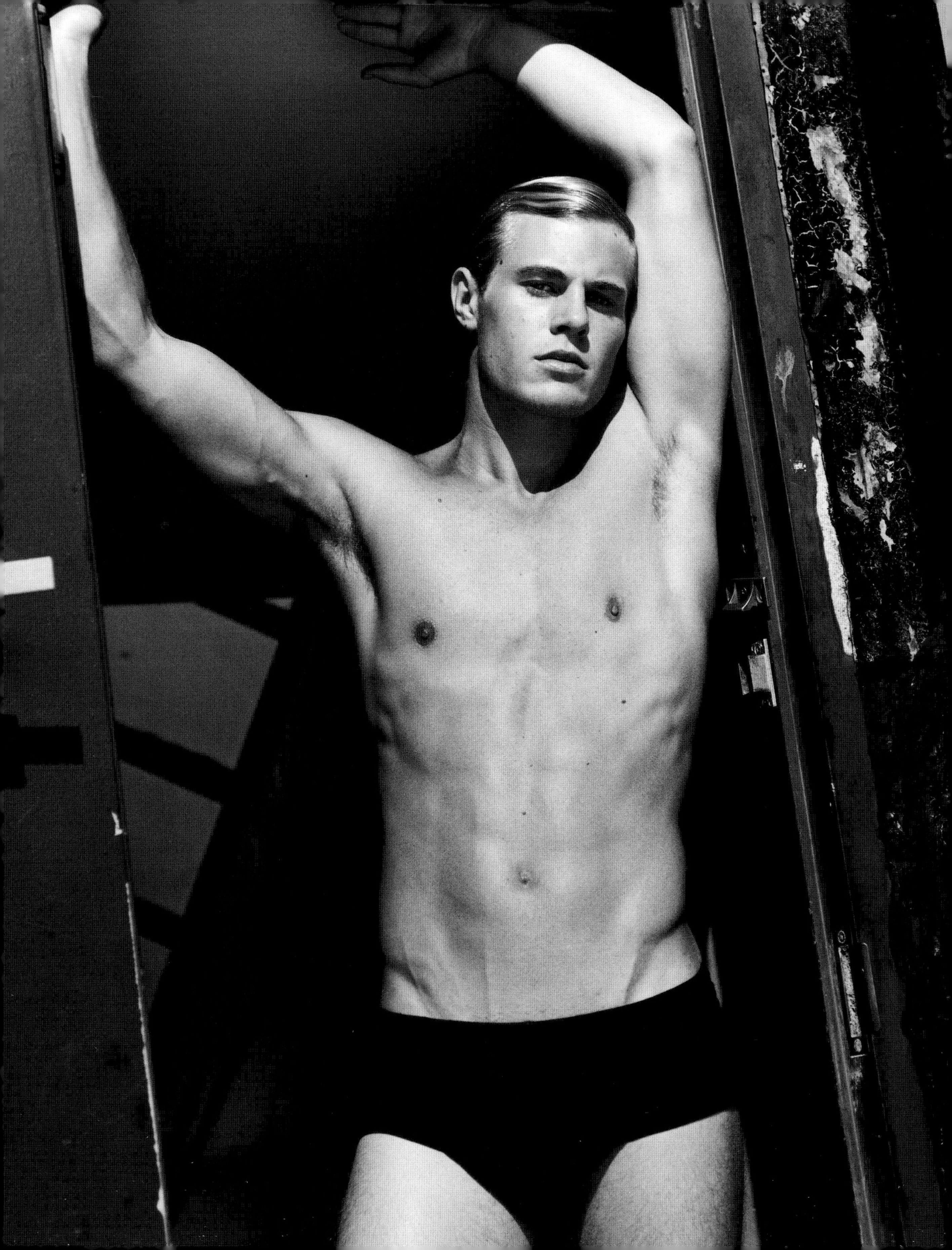

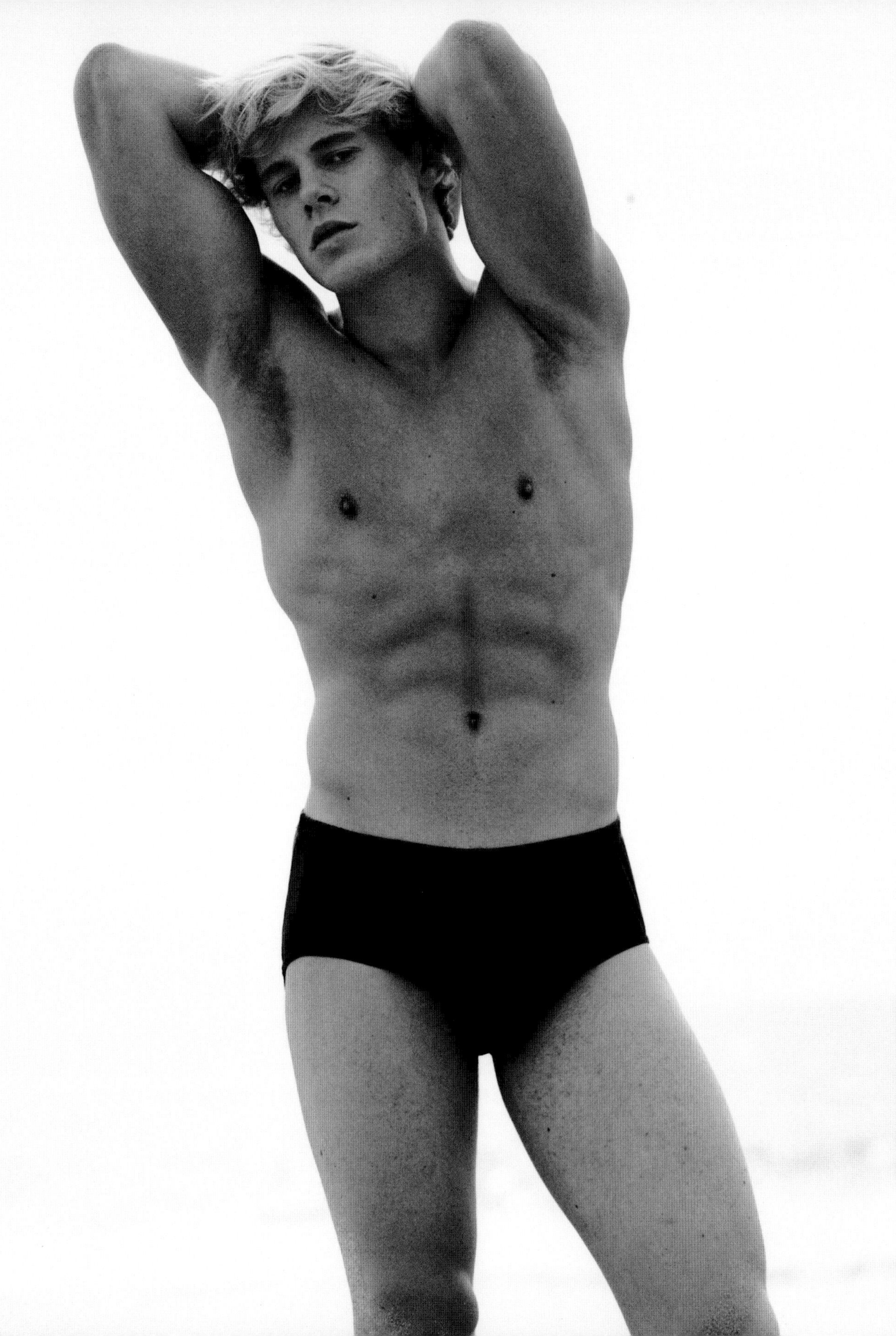

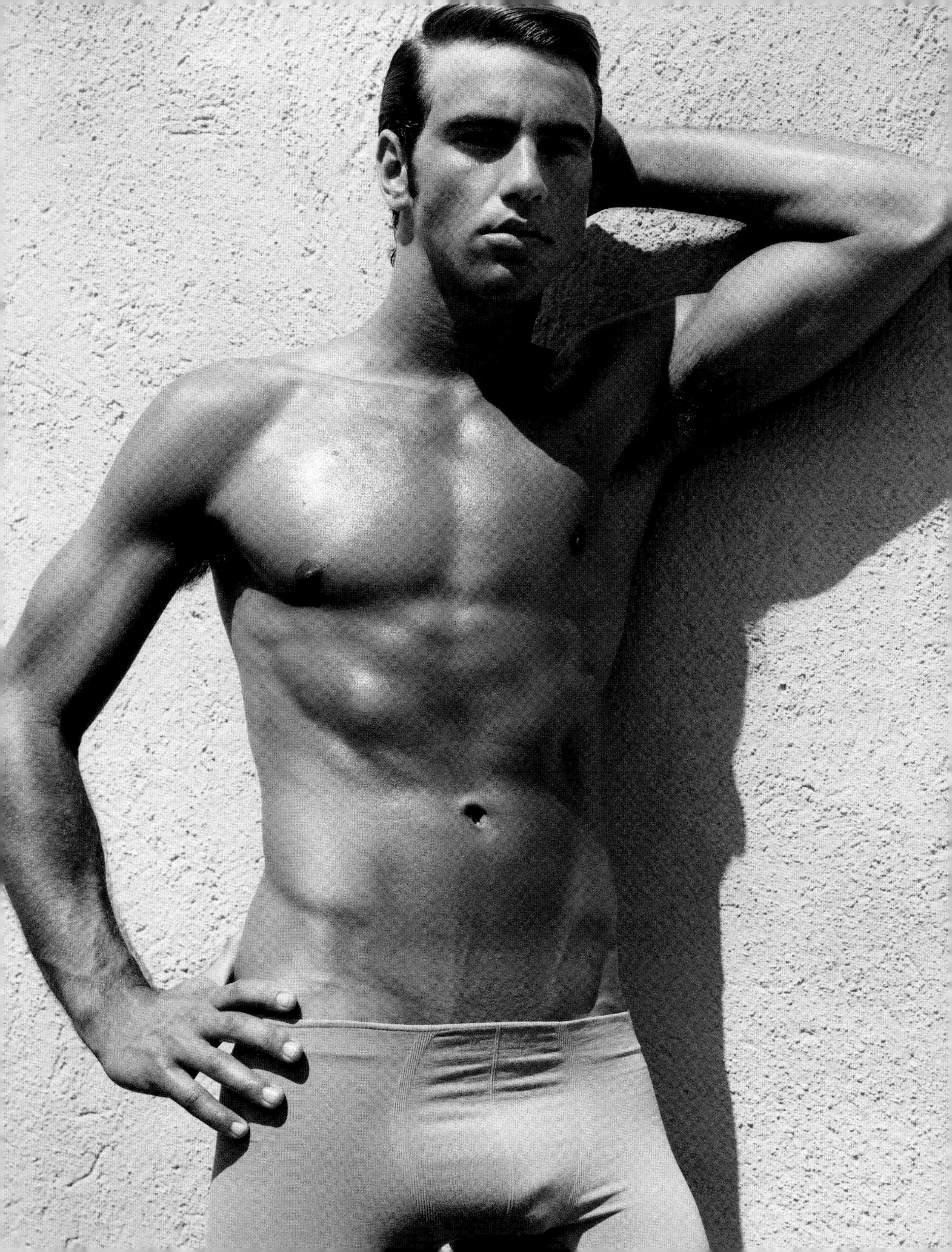

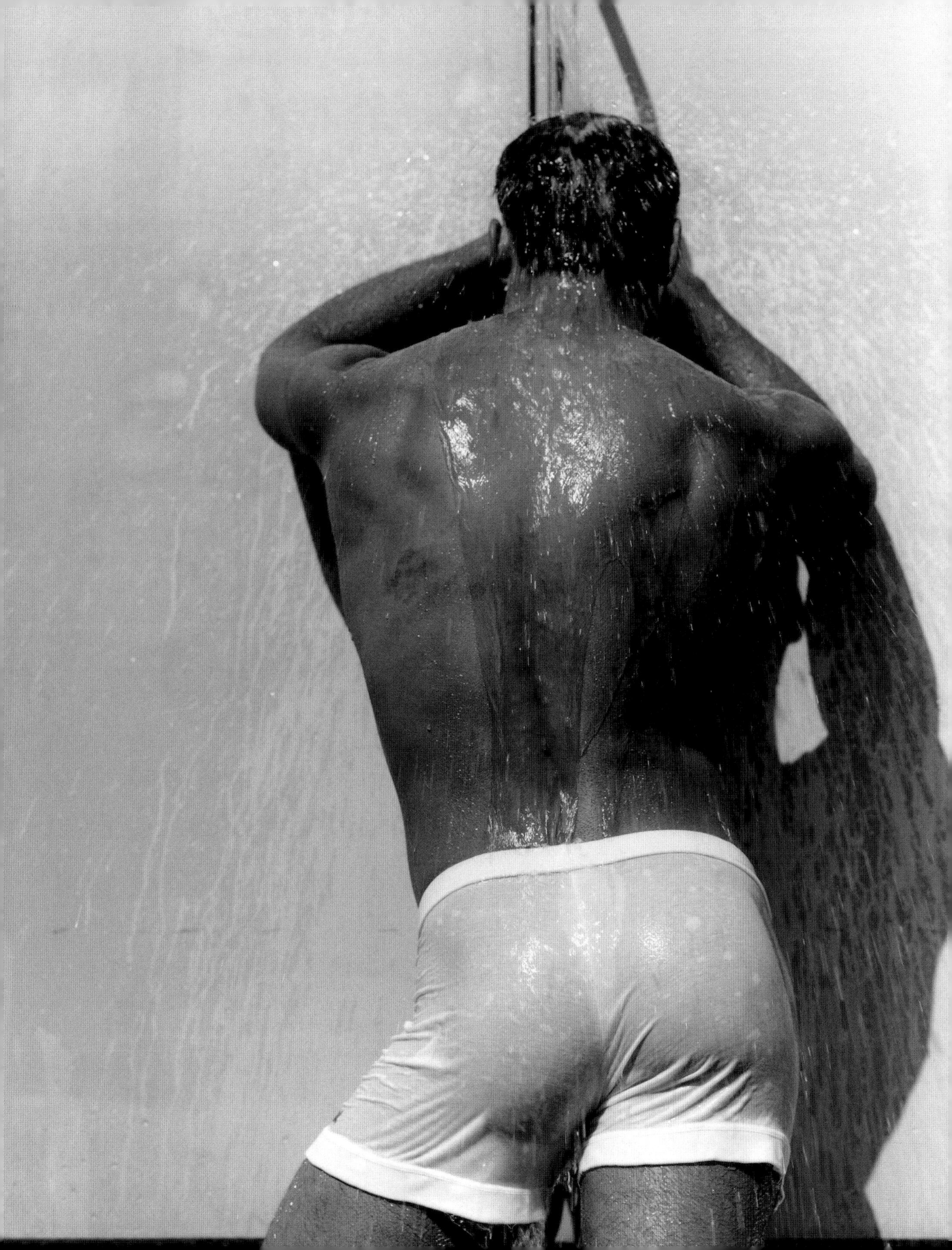

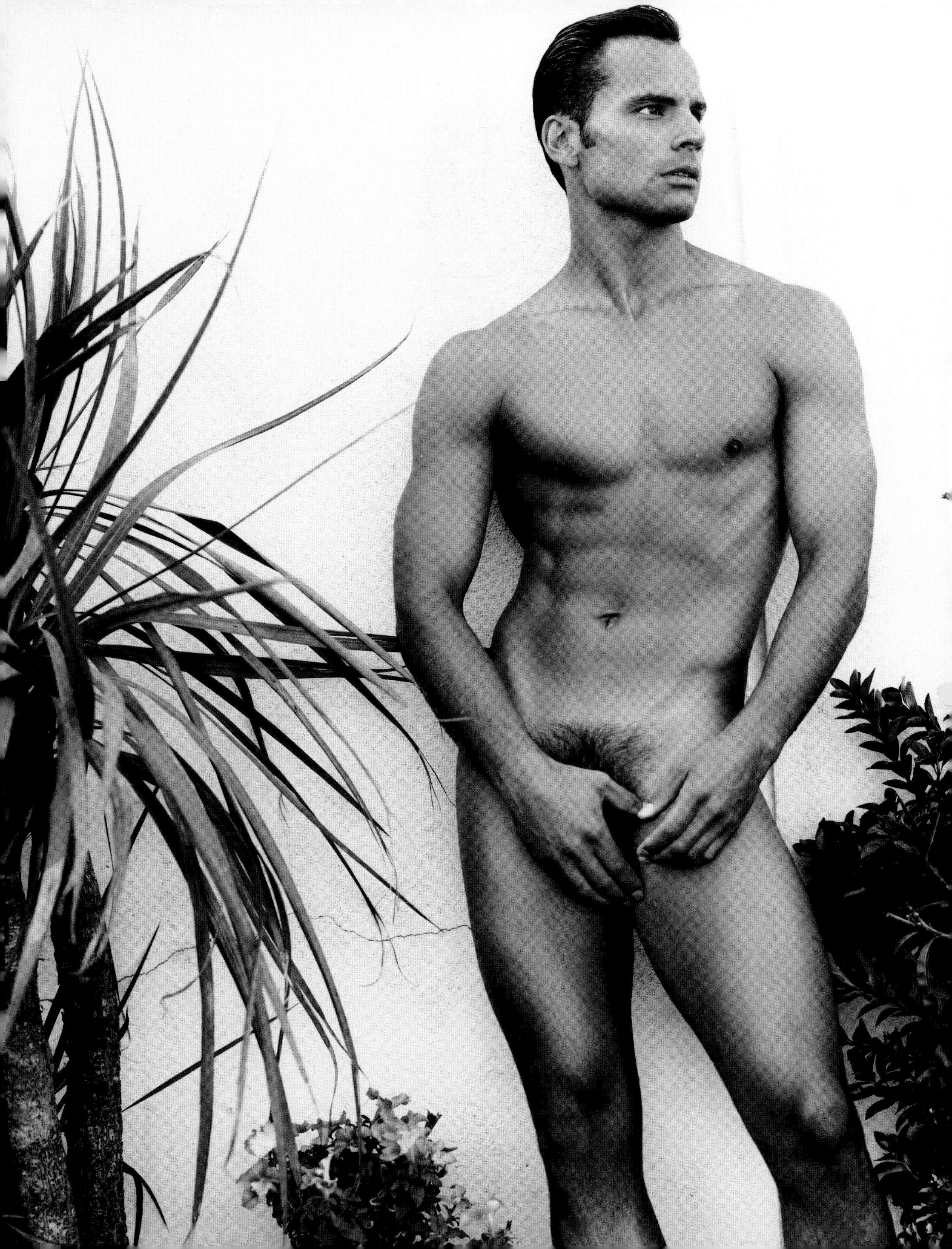

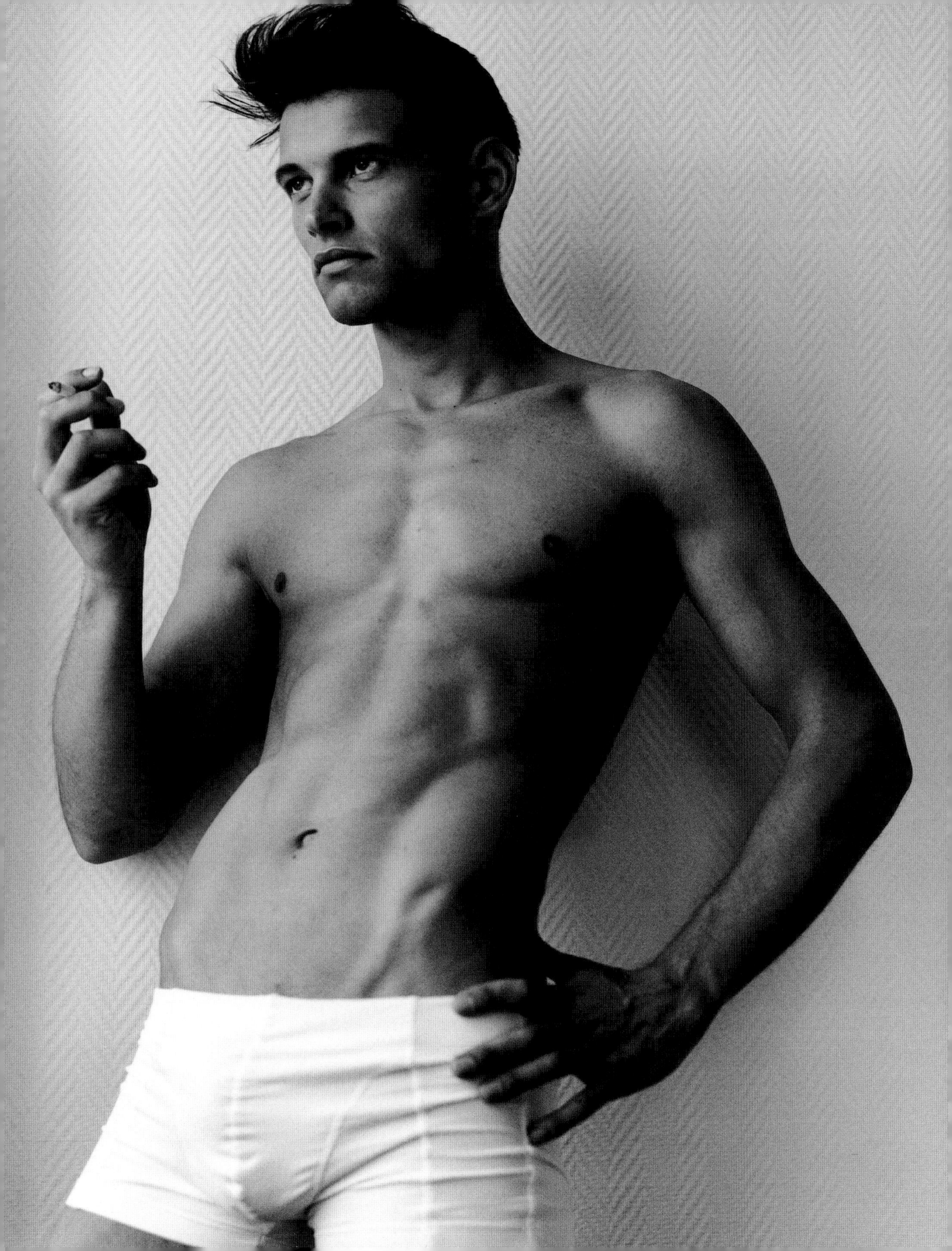

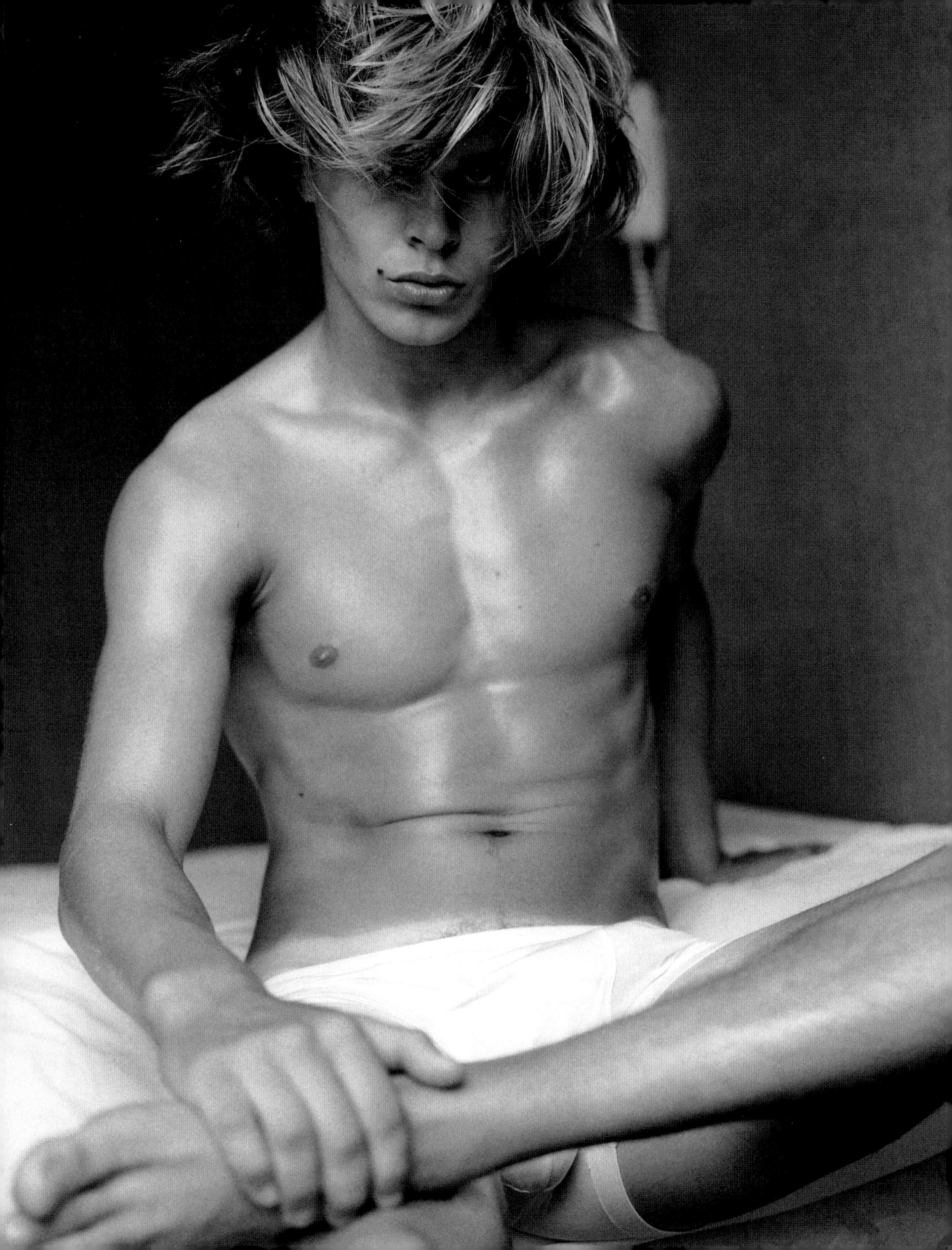

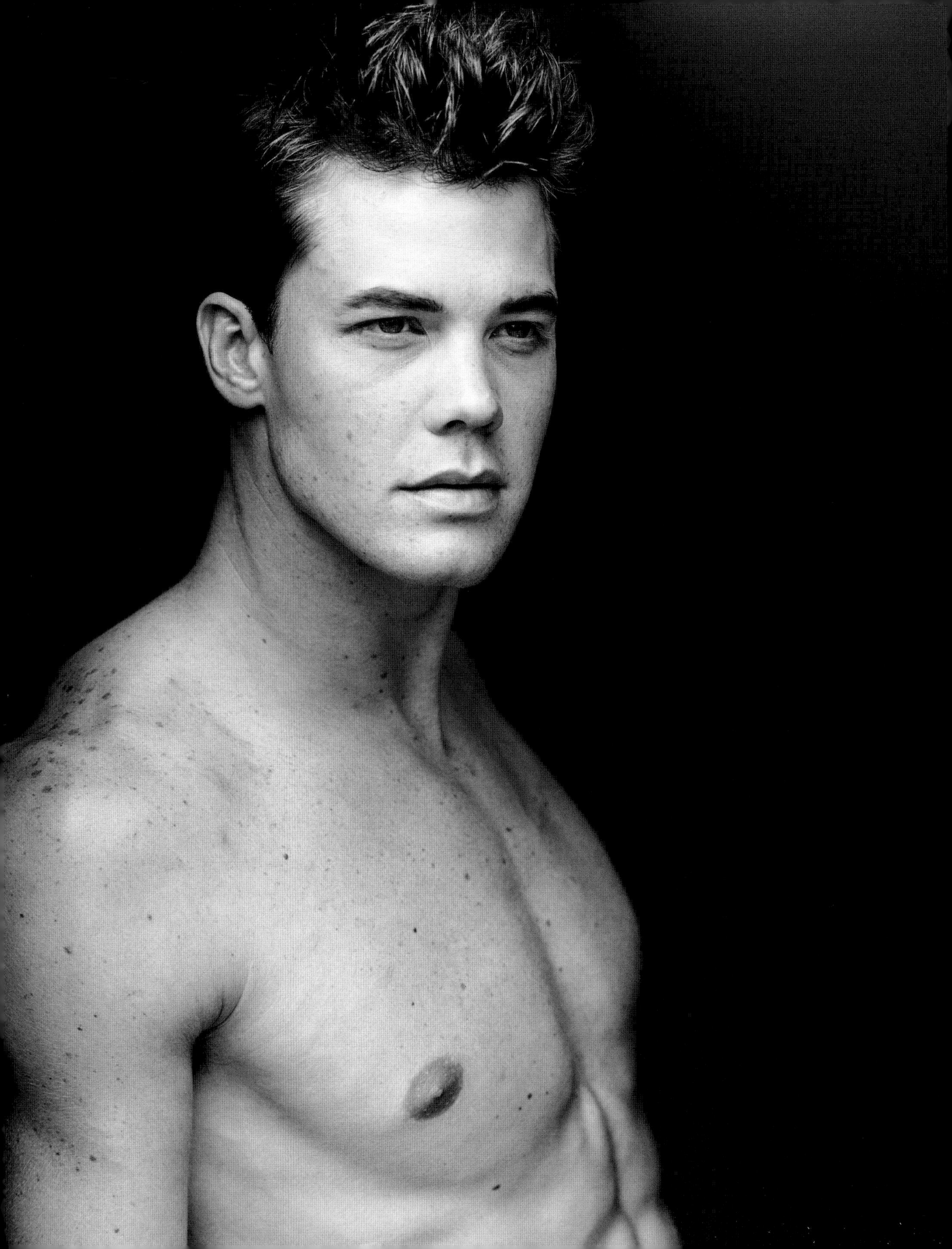

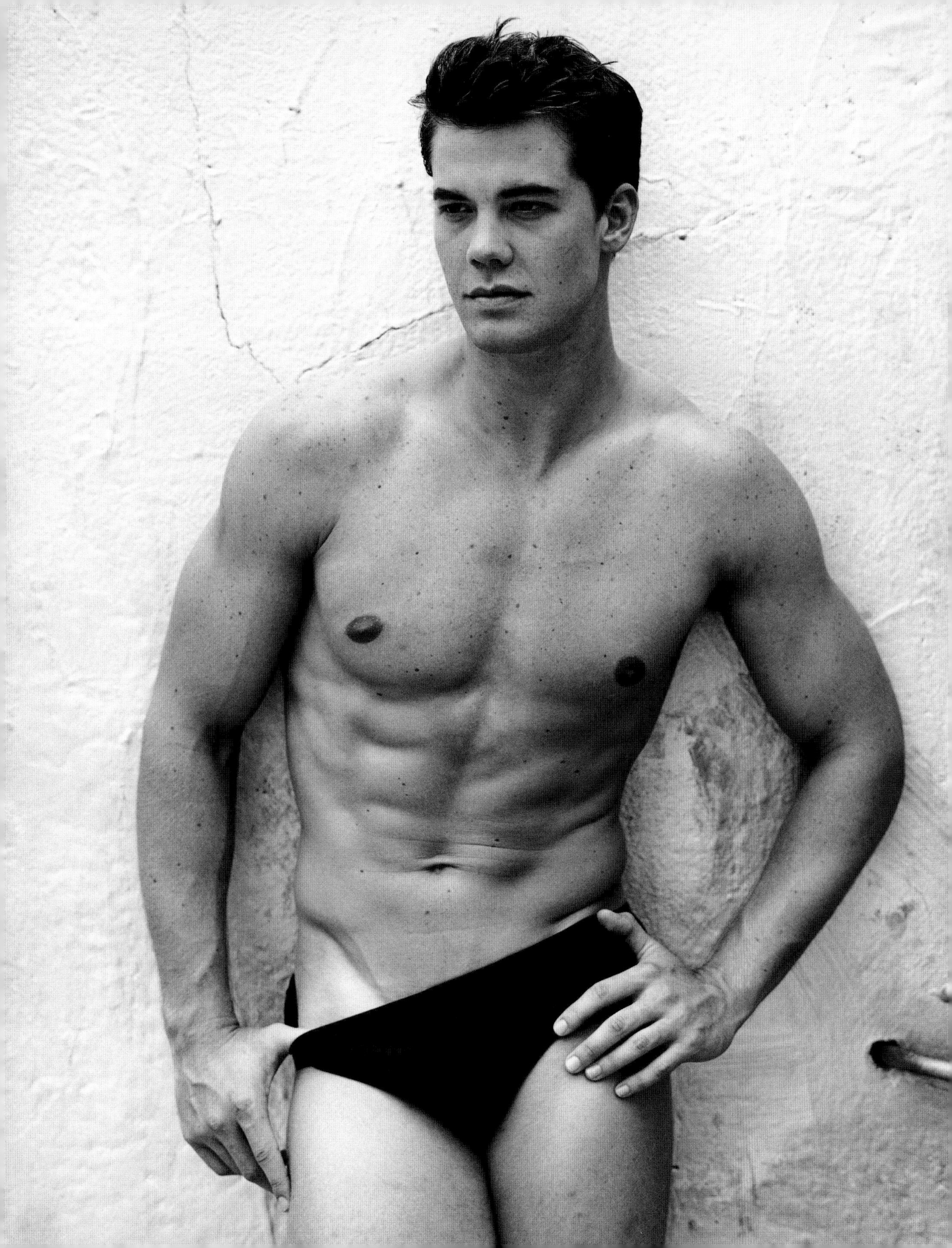

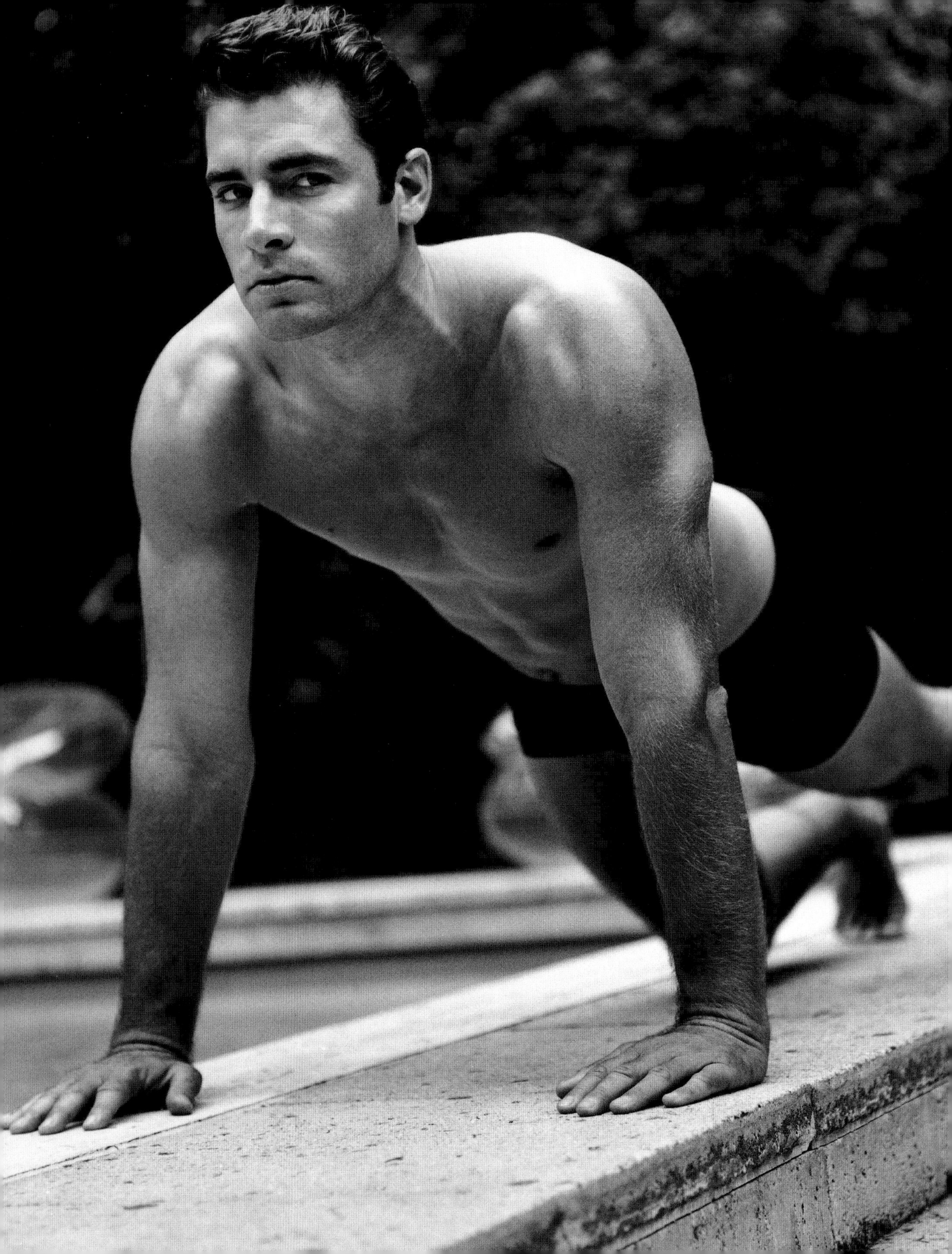

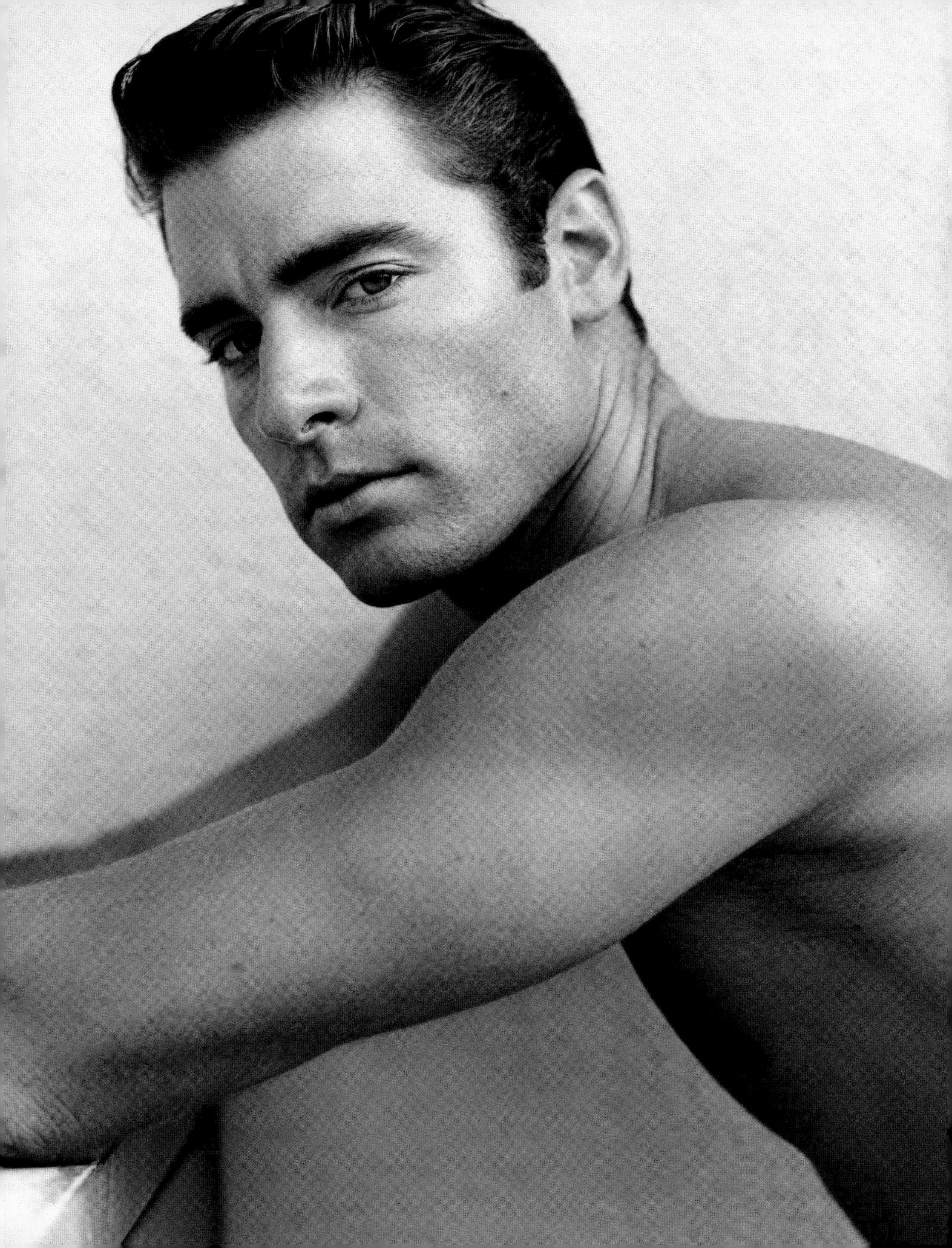

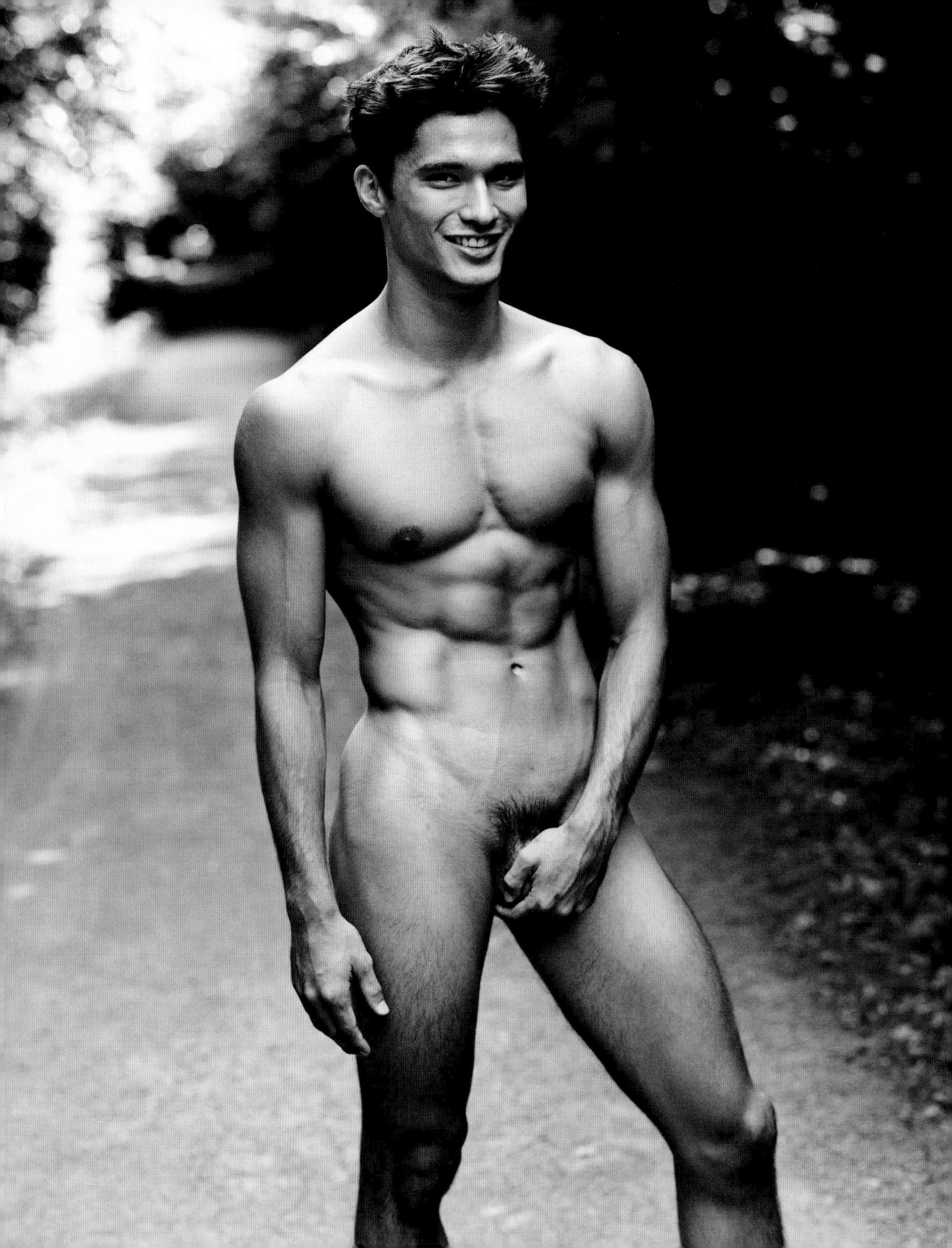

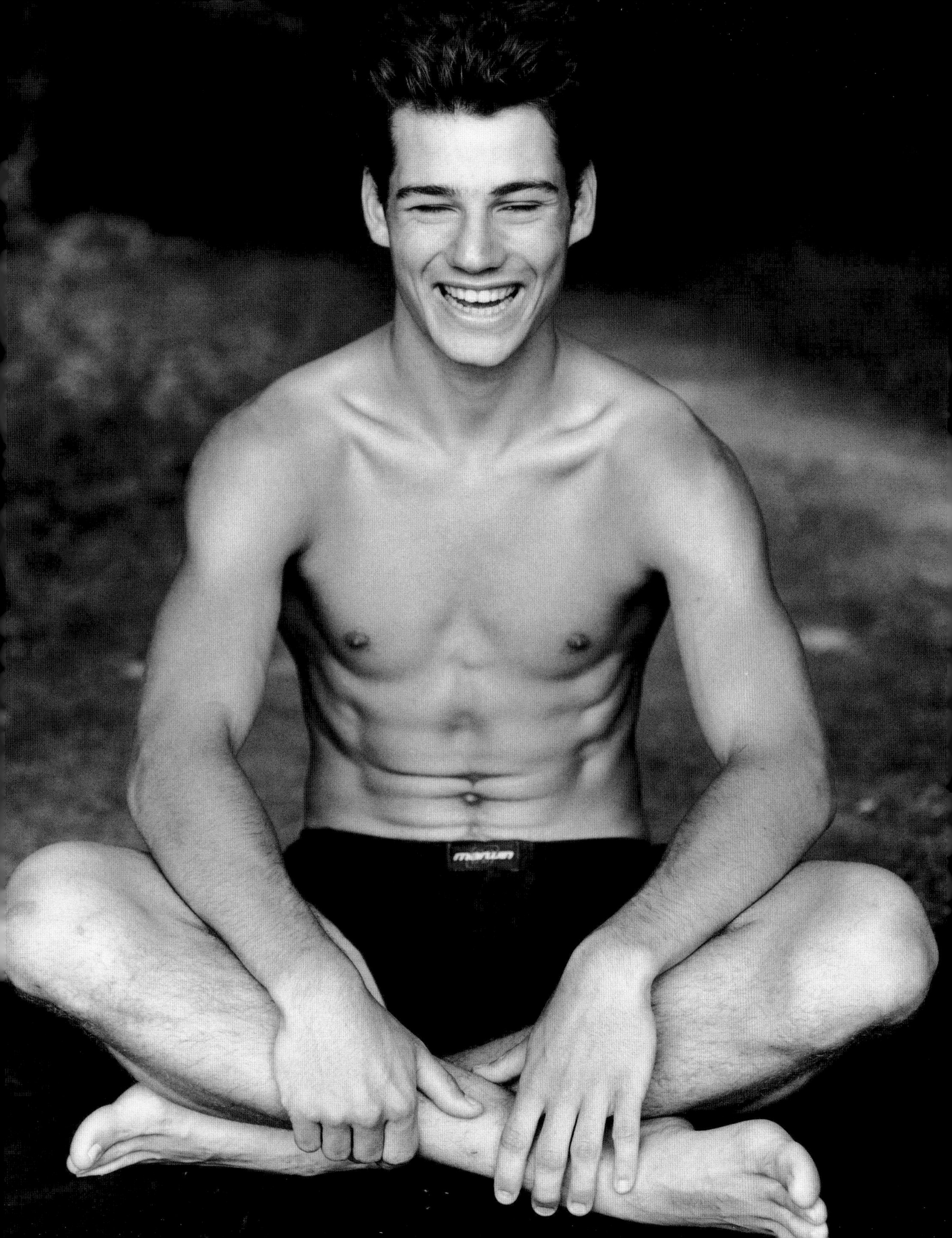

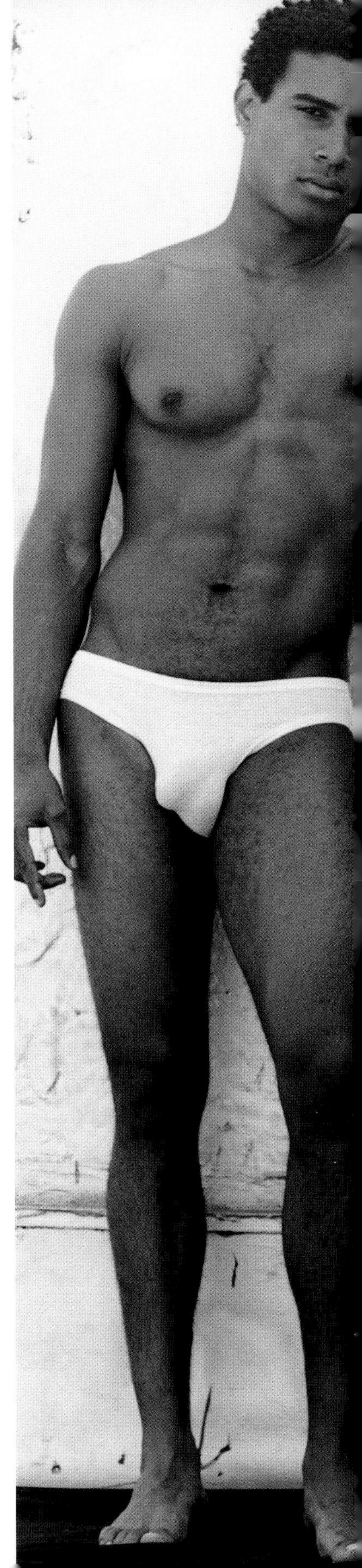

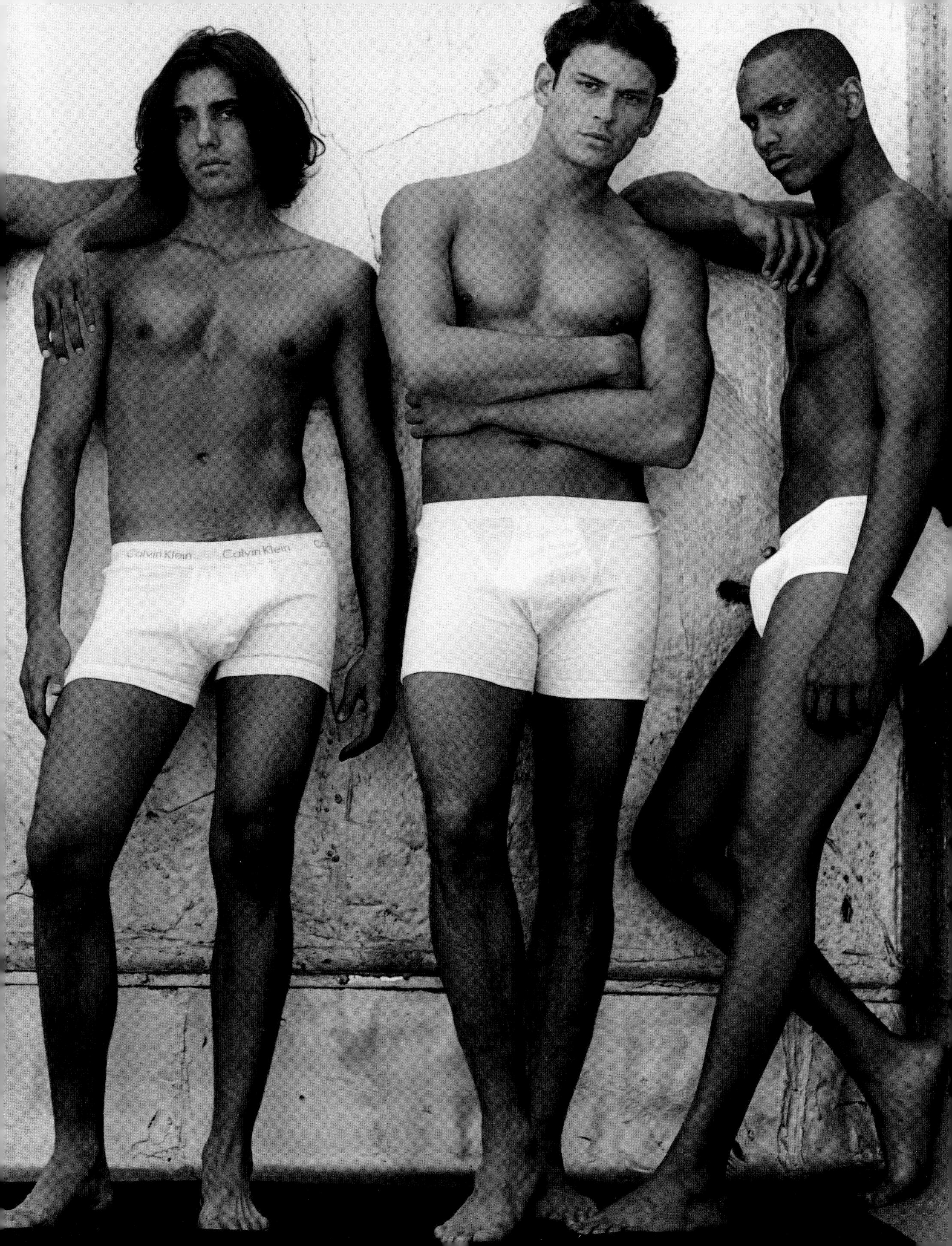

<table>
<tr><td>Cover:</td><td>Viktor, Barcelona 2003</td></tr>
<tr><td>Back cover:</td><td>Florian, Santorini 1999</td></tr>
<tr><td>pp. 10-11:</td><td>Roman, Miami 2003</td></tr>
<tr><td>p. 13:</td><td>Playa del Carmen 1999</td></tr>
<tr><td>p. 14:</td><td>Matt, Cancun 1999</td></tr>
<tr><td>p. 15:</td><td>Julian, Valencia 1999</td></tr>
<tr><td>pp. 17-24:</td><td>Florian, Santorini 1999</td></tr>
<tr><td>pp. 26-27:</td><td>Roman, Miami 2003</td></tr>
<tr><td>p. 28:</td><td>Arno de Jong, Barcelona 2003</td></tr>
<tr><td>p. 31:</td><td>Juan Alonso, Barcelona 2001</td></tr>
<tr><td>pp. 32-35:</td><td>Lanny, Bal Harbour 2002</td></tr>
<tr><td>pp. 36-37:</td><td>Matt, Playa del Carmen 1999</td></tr>
<tr><td>pp. 38-39:</td><td>Viktor, Barcelona 2003</td></tr>
<tr><td>pp. 40-43:</td><td>Victor, Barcelona 2003</td></tr>
<tr><td>p. 44:</td><td>Viktor, Barcelona 2003</td></tr>
<tr><td>pp. 46-47:</td><td>Tony, John, Jay & Christian, Barcelona 2003</td></tr>
<tr><td>pp. 48-49:</td><td>Sergio, Barcelona 2003</td></tr>
<tr><td>p. 50:</td><td>Miguel, Barcelona 2003</td></tr>
<tr><td>p. 51:</td><td>Toni, Barcelona 2003</td></tr>
<tr><td>p. 53:</td><td>Michael, Saint-Raphaël 2001</td></tr>
<tr><td>p. 54:</td><td>Torsten, Firenze 2001</td></tr>
<tr><td>p. 55:</td><td>Aydin, Barcelona 2003</td></tr>
<tr><td>p. 56:</td><td>Joel, New York 2002</td></tr>
<tr><td>p. 57:</td><td>Chris, New York 2002</td></tr>
<tr><td>p. 58:</td><td>Matthew, New York 2000</td></tr>
<tr><td>p. 59:</td><td>Lanny, New York 1999</td></tr>
<tr><td>p. 61:</td><td>Julius, Milan 1997</td></tr>
<tr><td>p. 62:</td><td>Tobi, Rodgau 1996</td></tr>
<tr><td>p. 63:</td><td>Michael, New York 1998</td></tr>
<tr><td>pp. 64-67:</td><td>Julian, Madrid 1999</td></tr>
<tr><td>p. 68:</td><td>Chad, Myrtle Beach 2002</td></tr>
<tr><td>p. 69:</td><td>Scott, New York 2002</td></tr>
</table>

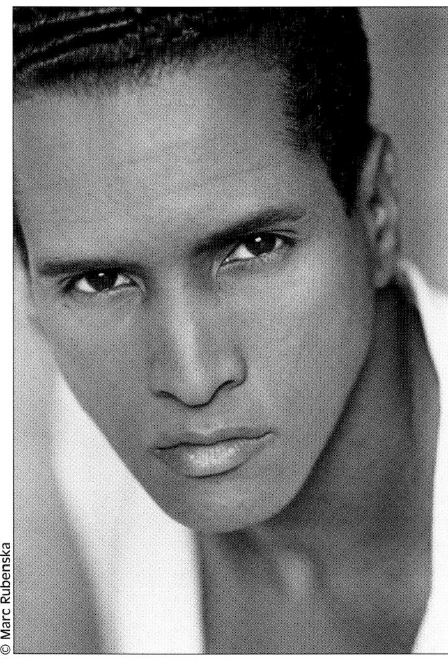

Born in New York City's Greenwich Village in 1959 Jeff Marano grew up no stranger to the artists scene. Living close by to actors and quite a few photography studios he could clearly remember sitting in on photo shoots of his mother Shirley. With countless magazines laying around in his parents apartment he could not escape the images of Avedon, Guy Bourdin, Hiro, Horst, Irving Penn, Lillian Bassman, Scavullo and Helmut Newton. That would set the stage for his interest in black and whites, which also made him more curious and left him in magazine shops on an almost daily basis.

It wasn't until summer 1983 that Marano realized the power of the "sexy male image" with Bruce Webers billboard of Tom Hintnaus in *Calvin Klein* underwear. At the same time legendary Herb Ritts played a major influence in Marano's career as Ritts shot him for a *Filenes* fashion shoot in June of the same year. It catapulted his modeling career and quietly sparked even more of an interest in photography. By summer 1989 while on assignment for Andrea Weidler's "Wiener Modellsekretariat" in Vienna/Austria Marano would catch glimpses of Tony Ward in the *Palmers* underwear advertising shot in Los Angeles by Herb Ritts. The billboards were plastered from the Westbahnhof to the Südbahnhof! The Ritts phenomena left impressions which would occur six years later. Marano picked up a Canon in a daylight studio in Amsterdam to help finish a portfolio test which the assigned photographer left unfinished. A few days later with the advice of famed Dutch photographer Jos Borsboom he bought a Nikon and started testing immediately. This was the beginning of this work in black & white. With Borsbooms encouragement Marano knew he was onto something! In no time he continued shooting body shots in Mexico, Morocco, Spain, France, Germany, Greece, Sweden and the USA and he built a repertoire of aesthetic and sexy images.

Marano jets between New York, Paris and Milan and his work is published in well-known magazines such as *GQ* (Portugal), *Men's Health en Español* (USA), *Cosmopolitan*, *AMICA*, *Qvest* (Germany), *black & white* and *blue* (Australia).

Jeff Marano wurde 1959 in die Künstlerszene von Greenwich Village, New York, hineingeboren. Er wuchs in der Nachbarschaft von Schauspielern und einiger Fotostudios auf und kann sich noch erinnern, wie er bei Shootings mit seiner Mutter Shirley zugesehen hat. Das Apartment seiner Eltern war voller Magazine mit Fotografien von Avedon, Guy Bourdin, Hiro, Horst, Irving Penn, Lillian Bassman, Scavullo und Helmut Newton, sodass er sich ihnen nicht entziehen konnte. Sein Interesse an der Schwarz-Weiß-Fotografie war geweckt, und seine Neugier trieb ihn fast täglich in Zeitschriftenläden.

Doch erst im Sommer 1983, mit dem Erscheinen von Bruce Webers Plakat, auf dem Tom Hintnaus für *Calvin-Klein*-Unterwäsche wirbt, wurde sich Marano der Wirkung des „sexy male image" bewusst. Zur gleichen Zeit beschleunigte der legendäre Herb Ritts Maranos Karriere, als er im Juni desselben Jahres Fotoaufnahmen von ihm für *Filenes* machte. Dies verhalf Marano zu einem Karriereschub als Model und heizte sein Interesse an der Fotografie noch weiter an. Im Sommer 1989 arbeitete Marano für Andrea Weidlers „Wiener Modellsekretariat". Bei diesem Aufenthalt in Wien konnte er mehr als nur einen Blick auf Tony Ward in der Werbung für *Palmers Underwear* werfen, den Herb Ritts in Los Angeles fotografiert hatte. Alle Werbeflächen zwischen Westbahnhof und Südbahnhof waren damit gepflastert! Die Eindrücke, die das Phänomen Herb Ritts hinterließ, machten sich sechs Jahre später bemerkbar. In einem Tageslicht-Studio in Amsterdam griff Marano zu einer Canon und half dabei, den Entwurf für ein Portfolio zu vervollständigen, den der damit beauftragte Fotograf nicht beendet hatte. Einige Tage später kaufte er sich auf den Rat des berühmten niederländischen Fotografen Jos Borsboom hin eine Nikon und begann sofort mit ihr zu experimentieren. Dies war der Beginn seiner Schwarz-Weiß-Fotografie. Durch Borsbooms Ermutigung wusste Marano, dass er etwas erreichen konnte. Er machte mit Aktaufnahmen in Mexiko, Marokko, Spanien, Frankreich, Deutschland, Griechenland, Schweden und den USA weiter und schuf ein Repertoire ästhetischer und erotischer Bilder.

Marano pendelt zwischen New York, Paris und Mailand, und seine Werke werden in namhaften Magazinen wie *GQ* (Portugal), *Men's Health en Español* (USA), *Cosmopolitan*, *AMICA*, *Qvest* (Deutschland), *black & white* und *blue* (Australien) veröffentlicht.

Jeff Marano est né en 1959 dans le milieu d'artistes de Greenwich Village, à New York. Il grandit dans le voisinage d'acteurs et aussi de studios de photos. Il se souvient encore des scènes de prises de vues avec sa mère Shirley. L'appartement de ses parents est rempli de magazines pleins de photos d'Avedon, de Guy Bourdin, de Hiro, de Horst, d'Irving Penn, de Lillian Bassman, de Scavullo et de Helmut Newton qui le fascinent déjà. Il découvre son intérêt pour la photographie noir et blanc et se rend presque tous les jours chez les marchands de journaux.

Mais c'est seulement en été 1983, lorsque paraît la publicité de Bruce Weber avec les sous-vêtements pour hommes de *Calvin Klein*, présentés par Tom Hintnaus, que Marano prend conscience de l'effet de la « sexy male image ». A la même époque, au mois de juin, le légendaire Herb Ritts fait des photos de lui pour *Filenes*, ce qui accélère la carrière de Marano. Cette rencontre donne un coup de pouce à sa carrière de mannequin et ne fait qu'aviver son intérêt pour la photo. En été 1989, Marano travaille pour l'agence d'Andrea Weidler, « Wiener Modellsekretariat ». Durant son séjour à Vienne, il découvre la publicité pour *Palmers Underwear* avec le mannequin Tony Ward que Herb Ritts a photographié à Los Angeles. Tous les panneaux publicitaires entre la gare de l'Ouest et la gare du Sud en étaient couverts. L'impact du phénomène Herb Ritts se fait ressentir six ans plus tard. Dans un studio, en lumière du jour, à Amsterdam, Marano prend une Canon et aide à finir un portfolio-test qu'un photographe n'a pas terminé. Quelques jours plus tard, il s'achète une Nikon, sur le conseil du célèbre photographe néerlandais Jos Borsboom, et commence tout de suite à expérimenter. C'est le début de son aventure photographique en noir et blanc. Avec les encouragements de Borsbooms, Marano sait qu'il est sur la bonne voie. Il continue sur sa lancée en photographiant des nus au Mexique, au Maroc, en Espagne, en France, en Allemagne, en Grèce, en Suède et aux Etats-Unis et constitue une collection de photos esthétiques et érotiques.

Marano vit entre New York, Paris et Milan et ses œuvres sont publiées dans des magazines de renom tels que *GQ* (Portugal), *Men's Health en Español* (USA), *Cosmopolitan*, *AMICA*, *Qvest* (Allemagne), *black & white* et *blue* (Australie).

Jeff Marano nació en 1959 dentro de la escena artística de Greenwich Village, New York. Creció en la vecindad de actores y también de algunos estudios fotográficos y todavía puede acordarse de cómo miraba shootings con su madre Shirley. El apartamento de sus padres estaba lleno de revistas con fotografías de Avedon, Guy Bourdin, Hiro, Horst, Irving Penn, Lillian Bassman, Scavullo y Helmut Newton de las que no pudo escapar. Su interés por la fotografía en blanco y negro se despertó y su curiosidad lo llevó casi a diario a las tiendas de revistas.

Pero no fue hasta el verano de 1983, con la aparición del cartel de Bruce Weber en el que Tom Hintnaus hace publicidad de la ropa interior de *Calvin Klein*, que Marano se volvió consciente del efecto del "sexy male image". Al mismo tiempo, el legendario Herb Ritts aceleró la carrera de Marano cuando, en junio del mismo año, realizó fotografías de él para *Filenes*. Esto ayudó a Marano a conseguir un impulso en su carrera como modelo y avivó todavía más su interés por la fotografía. En el verano de 1989, Marano trabajó para la "Wiener Modellsekretariat" de Andrea Weidler. Durante esta estancia en Viena pudo echar más de un sólo vistazo a la publicidad de ropa interior de *Palmers* con el modelo Tony Ward quien Herb Ritts había fotografiado en Los Angeles. ¡Todas las superficies publicitarias entre el Westbahnhof y el Südbahnhof estaban empapeladas con ella! Las impresiones que dejó el fenómeno Herb Ritts se hicieron notar seis años más tarde. En un estudio de luz natural en Ámsterdam, Marano agarró una Canon ayudando a completar el esbozo de una carpeta de fotos que el fotógrafo encargado de él no había terminado. Unos días más tarde se compró una Nikon por consejo del famoso fotógrafo holandés Jos Borsboom comenzando inmediatamente a experimentar con ella. Esto fue el principio de su fotografía en blanco y negro. Con los ánimos de Borsboom, Marano supo que podía alcanzar algo. Continuó con tomas de desnudos en México, Marruecos, España, Francia, Alemania, Grecia, Suecia y EEUU creando un repertorio de imágenes estéticas y eróticas.

Marano se mueve entre Nueva York, París y Milán y sus obras se publican en revistas de renombre como *GQ* (Portugal), *Men's Health en Español* (EEUU), *Cosmopolitan*, *AMICA*, *Qvest* (Alemania), *black & white* y *blue* (Australia).

Nato a New York, a Greenwich Village, nel 1959, Jeff Marano è cresciuto nel mondo degli artisti. Abitava vicino ad attori e a diversi studi fotografici e si ricorda benissimo che era spesso presente quando sua madre Shirley posava per delle foto. L'appartamento dei suoi genitori era pieno di riviste con fotografie di Avedon, Guy Bourdin, Hiro, Horst, Irving Penn, Lillian Bassman, Scavullo ed Helmut Newton, alle quali non poteva sfuggire. Nacque così il suo interesse per la fotografia in bianco e nero, che lo incuriosì e lo indusse a passare dall'edicola almeno una volta al giorno.

Ma fu solo nell'estate del 1983, quando apparve il poster pubblicitario di Bruce Weber su cui Tom Hintnaus posa per la biancheria intima di *Calvin Klein*, che Marano si rese conto dell'effetto che produce la "sexy male image". Contemporaneamente il leggendario Herb Ritts, ritraendo Marano per *Filenes* nel giugno del medesimo anno, diede una forte spinta alla sua carriera di modello ed accrebbe ulteriormente il suo interesse per la fotografia. Nell'estate del 1989 Marano lavorò per il "Wiener Modellsekretariat" di Andrea Weidler. Durante questo soggiorno viennese poté gettare ben più di un'occhiata alla pubblicità della collezione di intimo *Palmers*, per cui Tony Ward aveva posato a Los Angeles per Herb Ritts: tutti gli spazi per affissioni tra Westbahnhof e Südbahnhof ne erano tappezzati! Le impressioni suscitate dal fenomeno Herb Ritts si fecero notare sei anni dopo, quando in uno studio fotografico di Amsterdam Marano prese in mano una Canon per aiutare a finire un portfolio lasciato incompleto dal fotografo incaricato. Alcuni giorni più tardi, su consiglio del famoso fotografo olandese Jos Borsboom, si comprò una Nikon ed iniziò subito a provarla: fu l'inizio della sua fotografia in bianco e nero. Grazie all'incoraggiamento di Borsboom Marano sapeva che aveva la stoffa necessaria. Continuò fotografando nudi in Messico, Marocco, Spagna, Francia, Germania, Grecia, Svezia e negli Stati Uniti, creando un repertorio di immagini estetiche ed erotiche.

Marano vive tra New York, Parigi e Milano, e le sue opere sono pubblicate su rinomate riviste come *GQ* (Portogallo), *Men's Health en Español* (USA), *Cosmopolitan*, *AMICA*, *Qvest* (Germania), *black & white* e *blue* (Australia).

| **For your inspiring work** | Herb Ritts, Bruce Weber, Koto Bolofo, Michel Comte, Sante D'Orazio, Fabrizio Ferri, Brigitte Lacombe, Knut Bry, Steven Meisel, Mario Testino, Peter Lindbergh, Helmut Newton and Avedon. |

For your eye for detail

Juan (Shades), Nuria (Copia), Daniel (Premiere Vue), Frau Ziegler and Hanna (L+Z), Laurent and Laura (Lexington), Wim (Silverhands), Bob (New Move), Heide Müller (Leo Lab), Wolfgang Soeder (Grauwert), Frank Rilley (PPS), (Parolini), Randy and David (Dark Room), Birgit Schonges (Faco), Justin (68°), a big thank you to Rob (Arista) for getting me back on track after both of my portfolios were stolen.

And a big thank you to Vicky, Michael and Tree at Chelsea b+w for doing such a great job.
Your prints are great, Michael!

Photographic cards

Elizabeth Piantini (Print Ink), Patrice (T&P), Mario (RCA), Hans Dassen Produkties and Manuel Garcia Vilches (Trui).

For your support

Cookie, Wasse, Darren Johnson, Ari Vervelde, Dagmar, Sven Jaeger, Sascha, Hank Grimes, David Foley, David Osbourne, Dana Keith, Malcolm W., E. Lynn Harris, Tom O'Brien, Yancey, Roland Katz, Sam, Monika Leza, Mustafa, Kym Clark, Judith, Helen, Brigit Macklin, Lydia Tarsova, Tommy Garrett and Hans, Sandy Bass, Carol Miles, Jamie Foster, Pat Cleveland, Ralphy (†) and B'nard Jiles, Keith, Lynn Watts, Ros Johnson, Frankfurt Civil Service Boys, Anita Davis, Darryl, Jeroen, Tak Lee, Isabel and Pascal, Toshi Nakahara, Andrea Weidler, Marie Christine and Patrick Aubert, Pierre, Patrick Lavoix, Jouke, Peter Becker, Wilson Murphy, Ulf Siggurdsson, Gordon (Donnie) Reed, James Davis, Rita, Marjorie and John, Daniel Martin, Salvatore, Paolo, Alex Panzetta, Tom Morillo, Mika, Bruce Darnell, Karl Heitz, Ingrid, Andrew Van Wijn, Leon Holla, Tobi, Achim Hehn, Martin, Henrik the Swede!, Jordan Bewernick, Lanny Ward, Matt Janke, Chad Mureta, Be' Smeets, Bill Skinner, Donald Bauchner, Marcus Hartmann, Jason Ross, Rob Codner, Alex, Carlos, Paul, Tanya, Jay, Myra, Damaris, Jocelyn, Rosanna, Jeff, Dimi, Udo Landow, Rick Davies, Anton Eldridge, Kurt Knuts and family, Chris Geisenheyner, Lola, Madeleine Tuchendler, Alexander Spiropolous, Diane Washington, Ernest Collins, Lawrence, Iris Durie, Alwine Krebber, Sabine Scholz, Andrea Rehn, Aunt Myrtle, Aunt Dorothy, Aunt Evelyn and cousins Pat, Marie and Dorothy!

For your tremendous support

Aunt Marie and cousins Teresa and Elena, Bernd and Angela Koehler, Karin Koehler, Mario Windisch, Stefan Baumann, Holger Homann, Claudio Mauerhofer, Jos Borsboom, Ray Christian, Mr. Kermali, Rolf Stuggies, Kenny Gray, Tony and Lilly Houston and Steven Cutting "New York Fashion Designer"

Agents

Ron at Fusion, Noel at Request, Tim at Identities, Ray at Ford Commercial, Gary at McDonald Richards, Alvin at Model Service, Shane at ID, Oscar at "T" management, Jean Jaques, Roseanne, Paul, Renate, Marsha, Andrea and Normandy. — NEW YORK

Sonya at Crystal — PARIS

Carlotta at Fashion, Simona at Want, Christian Jacques and Val at Future, Daniella — MILAN

Fernando and Jana at Group, Carlos and Berta at Traffic, Carolina and Daniel at SS&M, Eva at Zutz, Montse at Salvador and Christina at L'Agencia — BARCELONA

Didier at Except Models — BRUSSELS

Gertjan at Max Models — ROTTERDAM

Nico at Kennon — DUSSELDORF

Wolf and Brook at Wolf Models — HAMBURG

And finally to EAST WEST MODELS in Frankfurt.
Thank you Marcus, Katja, Carlos, Helga and Andreas for being like a family!

And a big thank you to all of the models, sport students and boys next door for posing and being real for the camera. You all truly shined and made me as well! Especially the Barcelona crew. You were all *caliente*!

Magazines

Antonio at Men's Health en Español for giving me my first 5 covers.
Sabine Schulz, Immo Spieler and Matthias Held at German AMICA.
Robert Vescio at blue Australia for that beautiful gallery and Barbara Karpinski for that just perfect intro!!
To Stefano Carminati at Italian GQ for advertising my body book!

And thank you Mario Testino for your positive words of encouragement on that November day in L.A.

Last but not least to Ralf Daab for guiding me until October 2003 and introducing me to Hendrik teNeues, so EROS could be completed.

Thank you Mr. HENDRIK TENEUES for believing in me and my style.

Photographs by Jeffrey Marano, New York
Design by Iris Durie, teNeues Verlag
Introduction by Steven Cutting, New York
Translations by SAW Communications, Dr. Sabine A. Werner, Mainz
Ulrike Brandhorst (German), Dominique Le Pluart (French),
Dr. Nicoletta Negri (Italian), Gemma Correa-Buján (Spanish)
Editorial coordination by Sabine Scholz, teNeues Verlag
Production by Alwine Krebber, teNeues Verlag
Color separation by Medien Team-Vreden, Germany

Published by teNeues Publishing Group

teNeues Verlag GmbH + Co. KG
Am Selder 37
47906 Kempen, Germany
Phone: 0049-(0) 2152-916-0
Fax: 0049-(0) 2152-916-111
E-mail: books@teneues.de
Press department: arehn@teneues.de
Phone: 0049-(0)2152-916-202

teNeues Publishing Company
16 West 22nd Street
New York, N.Y. 10010, USA
Phone: 001-212-627-9090
Fax: 001-212-627-9511

teNeues Publishing UK Ltd.
P. O. Box 402
West Byfleet
KT14 7ZF, Great Britain
Phone: 0044-1932-40 35 09
Fax: 0044-1932-40 35 14

teNeues France S.A.R.L.
93, rue Bannier
45000 Orléans, France
Phone: 0033-2-38 54 10 71
Fax: 0033-2-38 62 53 40

www.teneues.com

While we strive for utmost precision in every detail, we cannot be held responsible
for any inaccuracies, neither for any subsequent loss or damage arising.

Bibliographic information published by Die Deutsche Bibliothek. Die Deutsche Bibliothek lists this publication in the
Deutsche Nationalbibliografie; detailed bibliographic data is available in the Internet at http://dnb.ddb.de.

ISBN 978-3-8327-9220-6

Printed in Italy

teNeues Publishing Group
Kempen
Düsseldorf
London
Madrid
Milan
Munich
New York
Paris

teNeues